Llewellyn's
2013
Witches'
Companion

An Almanac for Everyday Living

Llewellyn's 2013 Witches' Companion

ISBN 978-0-7387-1525-4

Art Director: Lynne Menturweck
Cover art © Tim Foley
Cover designer: Lynne Menturweck
Designer: Joanna Willis
Editor: Nicole Edman

Interior illustrations: Kathleen Edwards: 41, 42, 46, 85, 88, 90, 107, 109, 111, 134, 136, 138, 175, 226; Tim Foley: 9, 31, 34, 36, 81, 94, 97, 141, 166, 169, 172, 193, 202, 205, 208; Bri Hermanson: 61, 63, 68, 115, 117, 150, 153, 212, 216, 218, 220; Christa Marquez: 20, 25, 26, 75, 77, 122, 125, 128, 156, 159, 161, 197, 199, 231, 233; Rik Olson: 13, 50, 52, 55, 101, 145, 184, 187, 190, 236, 239, 240, 244.

Additional illustrations: Llewellyn Art Department

Any Internet references contained in this work are current at publication time, but the publisher cannot guarantee that a specific location will continue to be maintained.

You can order Llewellyn annuals and books from *New Worlds*, Llewellyn's magazine catalog. To request a free copy of the catalog, call toll-free 1-877-NEW-WRLD, or visit our website at http://www.llewellyn.com.

Printed in the United States of America

Llewellyn Worldwide Ltd.
2143 Wooddale Drive
Woodbury, MN 55125-2989
www.llewellyn.com

Contents

Community Forum

Provocative Opinions on Contemporary Topics

Witchy Living

Day-by-Day Witchcraft

Witchcraft Essentials

Practices, Rituals & Spells

Magical Transformations

Everything Old Is New Again

The Lunar Calendar

September 2012 to December 2013

Community Forum

PROVOCATIVE OPINIONS ON
CONTEMPORARY TOPICS

On Weather Magick

Eileen Holland

We are living in interesting times. Weather has been relatively stable for the past two thousand years, but climate change has come again to planet Earth. Accelerated by human activity, these escalating global effects are impossible to deny or ignore. Greenhouse gases are increasing, temperatures are warming, glaciers and polar icecaps are melting, sea levels are rising, and extreme weather events are more frequent.

As global weather changes, its adverse impact on humans will grow. Scientists predict that storms will increase and intensify in the coming years. Some places will get wetter, while others grow drier. Land will be lost as islands and coastal areas are submerged. Biodiversity will decrease but insects will thrive, possibly spreading diseases. There will be more heat waves, cold waves, and natural disasters like droughts, floods, and wildfires. Agriculture will be disrupted. There will be less fresh water as oceans grow more saline and increased competition for natural resources.

Climate change brings difficult challenges. Witches, with our special abilities, have to decide how to respond. We must choose between what we *can* do and what we *should* do. Is it better to ride things out, use weather magick, or do something else? Some Witches will disagree with me, which is absolutely fine, but I think that most weather magick is unwise or unnecessary—or both. I take a Babylonian view of the weather: let it be. I think we need to step back and take a hard look at the big picture before we consider using weather magick.

I think we need to step back and take a hard look at the big picture before we consider using weather magick.

Our planet is alive and constantly changing. This is clearly evident in the fossil remains of marine life found atop mountains. Even towering Mt. Everest, Goddess Mother of the World, was once a seabed. The Sahara Desert was once lush jungle, and it probably will be again at some point. Europe was once covered with ice and likely will be again. We humans may find it inconvenient, but geographic and climate changes are the norm for planet Earth.

All storms—including the wildest hurricanes, monsoons, blizzards, and tornadoes—are necessary natural forces. A healthy planet needs storms, and bad luck for us if we get in their way. (If there weren't so many of us, perhaps that wouldn't happen so often.) We should be sensible and realize there are places on this planet where people shouldn't live. If we can't survive floods, we should move off coasts and flood plains. We ought to know that it's risky to do things like build nuclear reactors on coasts or fault lines, and it's selfish to tamper with global weather patterns in order to protect lush waterfront properties.

Witches have special knowledge. We understand that Earth is more than a planet, more than just our home. Earth is Gaia, Mother Earth, a living goddess. She is wiser than we are and has made things as they are for good reason. We should respect her by respecting her creation. Mother Earth has been managing the weather for millions of years, and I think we should stay out of her way. Humans tend to see the trees rather than the whole forest. Working weather magick might meddle with her ozone layer repair plan, or her bring-on-an-ice-age-to-end-global-warming move. We are too small to understand what Gaia is up to, and we have no right to interfere. Humans should adapt to climate change, not try to manipulate it.

Ignorance and magick are a dangerous combination, and there is much that we still don't know about Earth. The Babylonians understood something that humans are only beginning to re-learn: that there are natural cycles on this planet. We have a fairly good understanding of several smaller cycles, like tides and the seasons, but there are grander climate and weather cycles that are more difficult to perceive or comprehend, like orbital cycles, the carbon cycle, and glacial/interglacial cycles. We only recently noticed the El Niño/La Niña cycle, and surely there are others we've yet to discover. Humans have a lot to learn before we're qualified to mess with the weather. We've just begun grasping the hard truth that we've damaged the environment by doing things like erecting seawalls, damming rivers, destroying wetlands, and containing forest fires.

Magick teaches us that everything is connected. When we begin to practice it, we also learn—often the hard way—that it can have unintended consequences. This is the greatest danger of weather magick: that it can inadvertently do harm. Imagine that a tornado or hurricane is bearing down on you. Of course you'd want to divert it, but think about the possible consequences: It might strike elsewhere and harm that place instead. If you do something like break up the storm or turn it out to sea, you might deprive an area of needed rain or set some other destructive chain of events in motion. There is much to consider.

So is weather magick ever appropriate? There is no one correct answer to this. It's a personal call, because every circumstance is different. It can also be a very difficult decision, because it's hard to see things clearly when we're in the midst of them. Divination tools, like runes and the tarot, can help, as can meditation.

Always be mindful that weather magick that disrupts agricultural cycles or Mother Nature's natural order of things is negative—chaos magick at best, black magick at worst. If you choose to work weather magick, you should exercise extreme caution. At the very least, include the intent or wording that the spell only manifest if it will do no harm. Being precise with wording and intent helps avoid unintended consequences . For example, you could ask Mother Nature (or the deity of your choice) to send rain, but only in the right amounts, at the right time, and to the places where it is needed. Spend some time working on your wording before you begin the spell. It's helpful to establish and maintain a relationship with a god/dess of rain, storms, wind, sunshine, and so on. Zeus is very reliable about sending rain. It's also important to work with Gaia, never against her, and to have respect for Nature. For instance, casting a spell to prevent beach erosion could entirely miss the point that it is the nature of sands to shift.

It's safest to eschew weather magick, but that doesn't mean sitting passively by when weather threatens you. We can practice other types of magick in those cases. For example, we can send positive energy to Mother Earth whenever we ground power and add thoughts about healing human damage to the environment. We are all different and should each work the magick that suits us. For me it's working with Isis to accelerate human evolution, because I think that's the best way to solve our problems. My glass is always half full, and I believe in human potential. If humans are more evolved, we'll adapt to climate changes instead of resisting them, and maybe we'll start to move inland, replace wetlands, clean up the oceans, find better ways to meet our energy needs, reduce pollution, and work on reversing past damage.

Even better, evolved humans could turn the problems of climate change into opportunities: cooperating instead of competing, and creating wondrous possibilities instead of clashing over dwindling land and resources. We would realize that we're smart and adaptable survivors who can use our hands and imaginations. We would dream big and exercise our options. Maybe we'll build domed cities, or engineer subterranean settlements, or create underwater cities. Maybe we will build spaceships and leave planet Earth, if need be. The sky's the limit, literally. There is, however, profound truth in the saying that wherever you go, there you are. Our future will only become better if we learn to live in harmony with the natural world around us.

Humans are fortunate. We're blessed with a blue planet—a water world of infinite beauty and variety—that provides us with everything we need. What have we done with this precious gift? We've strip-mined it, deforested it, fouled its oceans, and poisoned its air. We have exploded nuclear weapons, created acid rain, and hunted or crowded gorgeous animals to extinction. Perhaps we had better keep our hands and wands away from Mother Nature's weather cycles altogether. But we have been fools in the past, so it's never a bad idea to cast some version of a Protect Us From Ourselves Spell in place of any weather magick.

Eileen Holland *is a solitary eclectic Witch, a Wiccan priestess, and a poet. She calls her path Goddess Wicca.*

Illustrator: Rik Olson

Who Heals the Healers?

Calantirniel

Perhaps the title of this article ought to be "Who Heals and Counsels the Healers and Spiritual Counselors?" While it is intended for any who follows an Earth/Nature-based spirituality, it is also applicable for leaders and healers of what can be termed as alternative, New Age, or metaphysical pursuits, as well as teachers of any spiritually based discipline (yoga instructors are an excellent example). This is intended to be a starting point for a discussion that will hopefully arrive at a solution someday—other points of view are encouraged.

My Story

Inspiration to discuss this topic with others on similar pathways came to me over time. First, my Saturn Return approached me with a huge spiritual wakeup call—and a divorce to match. While working as a legal secretary and being a single mother of two young children—and somehow also learning astrology, tarot, and other astral, metaphysical, and divinatory arts—I was also "opening up" to those other dimensions, and I often did not know what was happening to me. You must take into account that I knew nearly nothing about psychic cleansing/hygiene and spiritual protection. While reading tons of books gave me a good foundation, I often found my new friends who had similar experiences were able to help me navigate the tough spiritual and astral territory. This became even more the case years later when I became a professional reader (and by then had professional friends), since I was opening myself even more—much more. It was extremely helpful to discuss observations made through our very diverse talents. Even though it often turned out that all of us were observing the same thing, I learned a lot through hearing about these additional viewpoints. I do not believe I would have reached the confidence level I've achieved were it not for these mind-opening discussions. I am grateful for these, and for the authors who took the time to write books so I could learn on that front as well.

More and more during this time of awakening, I was letting

While reading tons of books gave me a good foundation, I often found my new friends who had similar experiences were able to help me navigate the tough spiritual and astral territory.

go of society's conventional ways of making decisions and embracing choices that were empowering my new direction on an Earth-based, natural spiritual path. I was facing fears inside of myself, since the new choices appeared "risky," though I knew deep inside that the status quo was more risky as it meant the death of my soul. Even worse, I also had to stand strong and very grounded when challenged by others (family members, co-workers, and even authority figures) who were not open enough to understand my new choices. In the process, these people often believed I was crazy, and some tried hard to convince me of that.

Over the years, I have experienced many forms of energetic healing, through many therapies: Reiki, DNA Activation, Origin Constellation, Soul Retrieval, sweat lodges, and even other kinds of ritualized hands-on and distant healing. All these therapies played a role in correcting a small part of myself that was out of balance. Sometimes that role was to figure out when a so-called healer was completely full of it, which luckily didn't happen often. I often found that the best part of any healing is that it is automatically passed onto your kids! But I especially learned that healing energetic imbalances meant that a future physical problem could be eliminated before it happened, and thus energetic healing and physical healing are intertwined. I also learned that the current orthodox medical paradigm, due to its attempts to fight and control nature with unnatural methods, did not fit into my new belief system. And so I chose to stay away from this system as much as I could; however, I didn't know enough about alternatives at the time, so I ended up using mainstream methods more than I wanted.

Then, immediately after relocating from a large West Coast city to my small-town birth place, I had emergency surgery to remove my cysted right ovary and my very healthy appendix, starting a cycle of physical pain that rocked me to the core. It has been nearly eight years now, and since more problems have surfaced, I am still working very hard on physical healing. This learning process opened more doors: I became a Master Herbalist, further pursued flower essences, and became an Usui Reiki Master and reverend of the Universal Life Church. In other words, through experience, I was becoming a teacher and a leader and—most importantly—an example, which I take very seriously.

Now I am armed with newfound healing arts and am continuing work with trusted seers, medical intuitives, energy workers, a shamanic healer/astral "surgeon," and a gem of a homeopath who also does craniosacral therapy and psychic healing. I feel I am well on my way to staying out of the hospital and doctor's office! Herbal cleanses and diet improvements helped me, as did changing our drinking water to eliminate heavy minerals. On a physical level, I am clearing pre-cancerous fibroids/tumors without surgery (which involves having periods more often), eliminating my monthly three-day headaches that nothing seemed to ease, rebalancing my hormones, re-growing hair that had fallen out, breaking up scar tissue, clearing my skin, and even clearing issues of deep muscle pain. I learned this muscle pain was caused by bacteria and/or viruses going deep in the body, rather than just causing skin problems (something that I have always experienced). While I still have problems that need addressing, I am confident that staying on the homeopathic remedy will eventually correct all my negative symptoms!

While in the "birth" stage of my high-potency homeopathic remedy healing (marked by a scalp breakout that I hadn't had since birth), I also had a good portion of astral healing done. Some of it could be considered past-life contracts that are no longer relevant, but a lot of it was ancestral programming that transmits through genetics. I see why I needed to return to my small-town birth place (where some of my maternal relatives still live) to directly feel,

observe, and correct fear-based patterns that weren't even my own beliefs to begin with! These fears surfaced when I began living on the land, drinking the water, and breathing the air of my ancestors. I learned these imprints were not only ancestral, but they were still deeply ingrained in the people of my community. This programming is based on poverty-consciousness and the perceived safety of the group-mind, found in fundamental religion. Even though I have always been a creative and connected individual and always managed to create a certain level of prosperity rather effortlessly, I found I could only get so far in life, even with lots of hard work. Then, relocating to my birthplace, along with the surgery, had knocked out my creativity and connectedness entirely, which really brought this issue to my full attention. I astrally created a new right ovary and appendix so that at least my energetic system could work, and I asked Spirit to help me replace my connections to it, especially if these links had been accidentally "cut" with the surgeon's knife (it was an emergency surgery and my astral body may not have had time to prepare itself properly). Since anesthesia can leave you open for psychic attack, I needed to scan and correct any energetic imbalances that needed repair.

I share my lengthy story of personal physical and psychic healing with you so that you can follow and understand the following arguments about mainstream and alternative health care.

Some Observations

A new aspect of this topic came to me when I observed others who are in positions of leadership or teaching in a group that values being in alignment with the nature of Earth and/or the universe. These ideologies often instruct us to be in alignment with Nature— e.g., to use herbs when you have a cold, to realign our bodies with yoga to inspire healing energies, to use positive magic in rituals and bring about health and wholeness, to use energetic healing of the "All-That-Is" to heal a physical or other health problem—but what really happens when serious illness or injury is upon us? Most of us, in a state of fear and through our conditioning in society as well as family, will first go to an orthodox medical doctor. Even if the illness isn't serious, we often automatically choose to go to a drug store and purchase over-the-counter medicines, which are made with chemicals. Has anyone else noticed that these choices are not in alignment with a Nature-based philosophy?

I do not wish to eradicate the medical profession. There are indeed times we need medical doctors and their tools for life-and-death emergencies—a last resort, rather than a first. In giving this a great amount of thought, perhaps we seekers can model ourselves after our knowledgeable leaders to achieve natural healing. Unfortunately at this time, most leaders do not possess enough natural healing knowledge to be an adequate example; when they fall sick, they often drop the natural healing that they have been teaching in favor of expensive, invasive conventional medical care, which often fails for chronic conditions because it only manages disease and does not restore health. If our leaders cannot fully embrace natural healing, how can we have any hope for the seekers looking to embrace natural healing? And how did we get here?

If our leaders cannot fully embrace natural healing, how can we have any hope for the seekers looking to embrace natural healing?

What I also observed is that spiritual leaders in indigenous cultures were the ones who provided health and "medicine" to their people. While not everything could be cured, many things were—healings that even today cannot be explained and would be considered an outright miracle. These miracles still happen today in the tribes whose ancient structure is still intact. While we cannot duplicate an indigenous tribal structure in our modern world (nor would we necessarily want to), there must be valuable lessons to be learned from them. How can we apply such lessons to create natural healing opportunities for all who follow Nature-based paths?

The Dilemma

In looking more deeply into this issue, we should all realize we are not fully to blame. In the same way that Christianity worked for many hundreds of years to wipe out the Nature-based religious beliefs of the Western world, a similar process was happening to wipe out Nature-based healing practices, including herbalism, one of the oldest and most reliable healing practices. Many think that herbal medicine was prevalent only until the introduction of chemically derived drugs like aspirin, penicillin, and other antibiotics. However, in so-called developed countries, herbal medicine was always in the shadow of a poisonous metal that was mistakenly used as a cure for many hundreds of years: mercury. There have been long-term efforts to eliminate herbal knowledge on the basis of this one error, and these efforts almost succeeded.

In the height of the use of mercury for countless ailments (which actually harmed or killed many people), herbalism did experience a revival. By the time modern pharmaceuticals were starting to take hold during the later 1800s, a branch of Western herbalism (their practitioners were called the Eclectics) had mastered plant-based medicine at a very high level. This group was eliminated by the 1847 formation of the American Medical Association (AMA), which didn't like having competition for their short-term fixes that never addressed underlying causes. The AMA pushed out herbalism— and the few charlatans who really were peddling bogus cures—by lobbying to change laws; unfortunately, these laws are still in effect in the United States, making it illegal for anyone besides a medical doctor to diagnose and treat a health condition or disease. While other European countries have different legal issues with natural medicines, it is ironic that the United States—the country that promotes the idea of individual freedom—is the most difficult place to find real choices in natural health options.

Now, with the AMA and big pharmaceutical and chemical companies having so much influence over the Food and Drug Administration (FDA), change will not be likely for a long while. Because of this, even *information* about natural health is tightly controlled. If people knew that disease is often curable through natural means, they likely wouldn't spend all of their money on expensive doctors, hospitals, insurance, and drugs—particularly in light of the medical community's stance on incurable ailments and their lack of guarantees after these procedures and a lifetime of follow-up drugs. If information is featured in the news (like a study where garlic cures heart disease), a follow-up is featured nearly immediately with more "news" that discredits any natural remedy and deems it worthless. These efforts keep the general public confused and uninformed.

While herbalism only represents one part of natural healing's many options, the same can be generally said about other natural healing practices, whether they would be classified as a physical remedy or an energetic remedy. Reiki and acupuncture, also part of natural healing in the energetic spectrum, are actually making some excellent headway in mainstream treatments, and this is indeed encouraging—but it is not enough at this time.

So, now that we wish to embrace and implement natural means of healing, how do we bring it into our lives when it is basically illegal, and therefore unavailable?

Possible Solutions

While it may now be illegal to diagnose or treat illnesses without a medical license, we still have freedom of speech, and this can be exercised through the avenue of teaching. One excellent way of embracing Nature-based healing arts is to learn them. You can start out with books, exploring how the many hundreds of healing arts can all fit together. Later, when you feel an affinity for one or two (or several), investigate and pursue classes for achieving whatever level of that practice will bring about teaching opportunities. Once you begin teaching, you can still pursue even higher learning.

It may be a good idea to pursue one energetic method and one physical method and for them to be complementary—if possible— so that learning can be integrated. A third method could be in-between the other two, on the mental or psychological/counseling

level (astrology, for example), and a fourth method could be creative arts like music, painting, or dance. For instance, if yoga is a passion of yours (an energetic and physical healing art), pursue a type of teaching diploma and then study Ayurveda to go as far as you wish. If you already like Reiki and are drawn to shamanic healing, chakra balancing, and so on, pursue this and integrate it with something physical like Ayurveda, Chinese medicine, acupuncture, craniosacral therapy, massage, or yoga. However, if you find yourself drawn to several diverse practices, just go with it—you may discover a new way to integrate them into a unique practice.

If costs are an issue, manifest ways to do this training with rituals, asking for sources expected and unexpected; if Spirit also wishes for you to pursue training, the ways for manifestation will open up, whether it is work trade, scholarships, or an unexpected windfall. If you are confused as to what to learn first (doesn't it all look good?), you can use divination or ask for your first opportunity to reveal itself. Then be prepared to act on it!

In whatever you pursue, look into federal and state laws regulating your practice. For instance, some states will have laws that Reiki practitioners who do hands-on healing (touch) need to be licensed

as a massage therapist or be a reverend. For the states that allow it, applying as a reverend (or your chosen title) through the Universal Life Church can suffice. See www.ulchq.com for more information. If you can be accepted on a Native American Reservation as a healer, this opens up many more opportunities.

Knowing that you can't do it all, it is best to network not only with others who also do what you do, but with others who do what you don't do. For example, as an astrologer and herbalist, I located a local group of bodyworkers, mostly massage therapists, to trade services. We have found time-for-time arrangements work well, and if physical supplies are needed, we can trade them, pay for cost, or give more time to the supplier. Use your imagination.

It could be arranged that all members interested in healing ... explore and find diverse therapies to learn.

If you are in a spiritual group or coven already, it could be arranged that all members interested in healing (which is likely everyone) explore and find diverse therapies to learn. Each person can then teach and empower the other group members. Resources are more easily manifested in groups, as everyone can work together to attract what is needed. This will bring more knowledge to everyone involved and be the start of a network of healing. It is then possible to network and teach other covens and trade knowledge, which could start a chain reaction! While this is in no way an attempt to hamper divination arts or spiritual theory, my vision is that our spiritual groups are the first place we go for the deep, serious healing we seek. Our group leaders (and even other members) will then have knowledge and be empowered to exercise healing arts within the law and bring about the natural order of things—just as indigenous tribes do and have done since the beginning of time.

· · · · · · · · · · · ·

I look forward to further discussion about how we can make alternative healing methods more available and mainstream, since many more ideas, as well as new problems, need to be addressed. Please visit my blog and search for the post entitled "Who Heals the Healers?" While you are there, you can explore excellent online resources that I have collected over time. Thank you, and may all of you find deep healing!

RESOURCES

Griggs, Barbara. *Green Pharmacy—The History and Evolution of Western Herbal Medicine* (Second Edition). Rochester, VT: Healing Arts Press, 1997.

Calantirniel *has been published in over a dozen Llewellyn annuals and has practiced many forms of natural spirituality since the early 1990s. She is a professional astrologer, tarot card reader, dowser, flower essence creator and practitioner, and Usui Reiki Master, and became a ULC Reverend and a certified Master Herbalist in 2007. She has an organic garden, crochets professionally, and is co-creating* Tië eldaliéva, *meaning the Elven Path, a spiritual practice based upon the Elves' viewpoint in Professor J. R. R. Tolkien's Middle-Earth stories, particularly* The Silmarillion. *Please visit http://aartiana.wordpress.com for more information.*

Illustrator: Christa Marquez

Pagans & Cultural Appropriation

Lupa

When I was a newbie Pagan back in the mid-1990s, one of the first areas of belief and practice I gravitated toward was animal totemism. Along with Ted Andrews's ubiquitous *Animal-Speak*, I found a few dictionary-style books on "Native American totemism" and related "Native American spirituality." *This is so cool!* I thought at the time. Here I had the opportunity to learn genuine ancient nature traditions from real Indians! And it all seemed so easy, as I absorbed mythological meanings of North American mammals and birds, the Red and Black Roads, the Medicine Wheel, and how to apply these to everyday life.

I didn't recognize at the time that—like so many other nonindigenous people seeking spiritual answers—there was a fundamental disconnect between what I was reading and trying to practice and the roots of that material. It wasn't until years later that I began to think about the problems inherent in taking a society's cultural and spiritual practices out of their original context and trying to haphazardly apply them to my own. I didn't realize at the time that many of the authors whose works I was reading were not Native, and in fact often did not have official ties to any Native culture, even those whose teachings they were purportedly writing about. Some of them blatantly mixed New Age concepts like Atlantis in with a smattering of different tribes' lore and called it "genuine Native spirituality." There were people deliberately misrepresenting themselves and the sources of their teachings, or at the very least not correcting their audience's misconceptions about how "Native" they themselves were (or weren't).

But people were eating it up anyway and apparently getting a lot of fulfillment out of the material, misrepresentation or not. While I drifted away from those things into my own self-directed practice, I found myself confronting a salient issue again and again: cultural appropriation.

Killing the Tree at the Root

Cultural appropriation is taking elements of another culture (including spiritual aspects), generally one that is less powerful than your own, and using them for your own ends. Although cultures have historically borrowed from and been inspired by each other for millennia, the concept of cultural appropriation has a negative connotation in that the borrowing is often harmful to the culture being taken from. Racism, whether overt or not, is a common element, and the borrowing is very often done in ignorance of other, more significant damages done to the borrowed-from by the borrower.

Take Native American cultures, for example. One of the very best classics of Native American history is Dee Brown's *Bury My Heart at Wounded Knee*. The first time I read it, the impression I had was that each chapter was the same story told over and over again with a different set of tribes each time. White people would approach the tribes, maybe threaten them, create a treaty, break the treaty, and refuse to negotiate with the Indians, instead enacting genocide upon them. And that hasn't ended. Today reservations are among the very poorest places in the United States, and the addiction, poverty, and crime rates among Native Americans are exceedingly high compared to other racial and cultural groups. Far too many white Americans view Native Americans as a lesser race, as a piece of the past

and invisible in modern times—or as "noble savages" waiting to impart great wisdom on eager white hippies.

Many, if not most, of the people who claim to practice "Native American shamanism" seem to ignore this reality. A popular magazine for shamanic practitioners is stuffed full of advertisements for expensive trips to South American locales to learn "from real shamans!" Not mentioned is the fact that many of the destinations are poverty-stricken communities, often in danger from autocratic non-indigenous governments, drug wars, and natural disasters like drought or floods.

And yet despite this reality, people continue to blithely buy books and go to seminars on "Native American spirituality" without understanding that very little of their money goes to benefit the cultures whose teachings may have been bastardized in the process. The few true indigenous elders who are willing to reach out beyond their communities are often overshadowed by non-Native impostors.

The taking of spirituality and other cultural elements is just the latest iteration of cultural genocide. The harsh realities of poverty and addiction are ignored in favor of the image of people close to the land, living ancient traditions. While the traditions may live on in genuine cultural practices such as pow wows and tribe-specific rites, only appreciating indigenous cultures for their spirituality (what we perceive of it anyway) contributes to a candy-coated view of them not as people, but as only sources for our spiritual gratification.

Taking Cultural Context into Consideration

One of the arguments I see for continuing to utilize appropriated material—whether from Native American cultures, African Diaspora religions such as Vodou or Santería, or other disadvantaged groups—is that "Spirituality is free! If the gods/lwa/totems/etc. come to me, I have to answer!" The latter may be true, and far be it from me to tell someone to ignore the call of a deity or spirit from another culture. However, the exact practices of a particular spirituality are not necessarily meant to be free for the taking.

It may seem appropriate to use Native American rituals and other practices to connect with land spirits in the United States, especially when many non-indigenous (especially white) Americans feel that their own culture is spiritually empty. After all, when in Washington, do as the Salish do, right? Not necessarily. Human beings are not "plug and play" when it comes to culture. Most of us cannot just step into a new culture and feel instantly at home, and fewer still will be welcomed by its Natives with open arms.

Spiritual practices do not develop in a vacuum. Contrary to the claims of many neoshamans, there is no such thing as being "culturally neutral." You cannot do anything without your culture of origin (and current culture, if different) coming into play. From birth we learn from our cultures how to act, communicate, think, learn, believe, etc. We are immersed in culture. Most neoshamanisms, rather than being "culturally neutral," are based primarily in white, middle-class, college-educated cultural perspectives. While Michael Harner, for example, based core shamanism in his experiences with the Jivaro and other indigenous cultures, core shamanism appeals directly to his culture of origin as a white, middle-class academic professor.

> **Contrary to the claims of many neoshamans, there is no such thing as being "culturally neutral."**

Confronting Our Privilege

As a similar white, middle-class person with an academic history, I am well aware of my privilege. The concept of privilege is designed to help people be aware of where they may have advantages over others by virtue not of personal effort, but of inherent factors like race, socio-economic status, and so on. Privilege does not make one immune from suffering or problems or from lacking privilege in other areas. It is simply a way to create awareness that there is no level playing field, and that some people come into this world with more resources and fewer barriers than others.

The ignorance of many white neoshamans toward the sad reality of impoverished, oppressed indigenous communities is a prime example of privilege. Some people have the ability to ignore these

problems; that's part of their privilege. The indigenous people don't have that luxury. And the same goes for the genocide, the continual environmental devastation on Native lands (what's left of them, anyway), and the taking of indigenous teachings.

The initial reaction to realizing that you may be one of these seemingly clueless people may be to get defensive, or perhaps to feel guilty. You may try to say "Well, I'm not privileged, because I experienced this and that and the other …" Or you may beat yourself up with guilt and shame and feel like a horrible person. Both of these responses are counterproductive, because they still turn your attention (and that of others) on you. While how you feel is certainly valid, the key to confronting privilege is to not let it turn you even further inward on yourself; that sort of blindness to others' problems is what started these problems in the first place.

Instead, turn your attention outward. Listen to the criticisms, even if they hurt. If you can, try to have constructive dialogue with people of disadvantaged groups to try to understand where they're coming from, or at the very least find their writings online and in books, when possible, to start hearing their authentic voices. The reality of oppressed people very often is defined by the majority population ignoring them. By being able to open your ears to what they have to say, without defensiveness or guilt, you can help turn the tide, even just a little.

On a spiritual level, this may mean researching the reactions of those cultures whose practices you may be interested in or even implementing yourself. For example, New Age Frauds and Plastic Shamans, located at http://www.newagefraud.org, is one hub for information on appropriation of Native American cultural elements. Racialicious.com frequently highlights issues of spiritual appropriation from numerous cultures. And Googling "cultural appropriation and spirituality" brings up a wealth of research material.

But I Want to Be a Shaman Anyway!

Let's say that in spite of all this, you're a white person who wants to be a shaman, or a Vodouisant, or maybe just integrate a little bit of Chinese medicine into your life. While all the aforementioned research material may be helpful in gaining an intellectual understanding of the concept, the truest test comes when you explore your own practices and motivations according to what you've learned. From there you can approach your choices with more honesty and conscious awareness. Here are a few starting points:

- First, ask yourself why you want to practice the path that you are interested in. Do you have a realistic view of what it's about, or are your notions largely romanticized? Do you feel that you

must follow someone else's creation in order to connect with the land, the spirits, etc.? Do you know someone else who practices it, and it seemed interesting to you?

- Do you have any connections to the culture itself? If not, is reliable information readily available to curious outsiders? Is the culture hostile to newcomers, and if so, why?

- Do you just want the spiritual trappings, or are you interested in getting to know the culture as a whole? Are you okay with the possibility that this may take years or even decades? Are you willing to explore potential areas of privilege you may have in comparison to people from the culture?

- Are you interested in alternatives that may be more accessible to you? What about creating your own path based in your own cultural experiences (though perhaps being responsibly inspired by others' paths)?

What does "responsibly inspired" mean, anyway? In short, it's carefully adopting elements of another culture's practices for yourself, either directly or as inspiration for your own, while being aware that you are changing those processes by the very act of borrowing them. It's doing so with the awareness that even despite your best intent, there may be people who feel harmed by your decisions. It's remembering that using a few bits and pieces of a culture does not mean you are a part of that culture, nor do you understand that culture in its entirety, without romanticism or racism. It also means periodically checking your conscience, and perhaps getting feedback from other people, Pagans and otherwise, about what you're doing. And it's accepting that there may simply be places you are unable to go with your spirituality, and that it is better to let them go than to force your way in.

Blazing Your Own Trail

Early on, I thought the books on "Native American spirituality" were just fine to take in without questioning. These days I know better. I'm a lot more skeptical, and the shamanic path that I've been developing is consciously based in my experiences as a white, middle-class, college-educated woman with a lot of experience in Neopaganism. And it works better for me than anything else has.

One thing I learned is that you don't have to use the practices and language of a deity or spirit's native culture in order to work with them. In addition to numerous animal totems and local land spirits, I have worked with Artemis, Anubis, and other deities from around the world. In each case, I created my own ways of working with them in ritual and in offering. If it is more harmful to try to appropriate

Native practices, or if you simply feel more comfortable doing things your own way, nothing says you can't be just as successful.

Spirituality isn't about doing things the way everyone else does, just because that's how other people do it; it's about creating your own relationships with the powers that be, however that works most effectively.

RESOURCES

Brown, Dee. *Bury My Heart at Wounded Knee: An Indian History of the American West,* 30th Anniversary edition. New York: Holt Paperbacks., 2001.

Lupa, ed. *Talking about the Elephant: An Anthology of NeoPagan Perspectives on Cultural Appropriation.* Stafford: Immanion Press/Megalithica Books, 2007.

Lupa. *Therioshamanism: Cultural Appropriation.* (2007–2011) http://therio shamanism.com/category/cultural-appropriation/

McIntosh, Peggy. *White Privilege: Unpacking the Invisible Knapsack.* (1988) http://www.nymbp.org/reference/WhitePrivilege.pdf

New Age. "Frauds and Plastic Shamans." http://www.newagefraud.org

Ziff, Bruce, and Pratima V. Rao, eds. *Borrowed Power: Essays on Cultural Appropriation.* New Brunswick: Rutgers University Press, 1997.

Lupa *is a (neo)shaman, author, artist, and professional counselor living in Portland, Oregon. She is the author of several books on neoshamanism and related topics, including* New Paths to Animal Totems *(Llewellyn, 2012). When she isn't attacking the computer keyboard or making ritual tools out of dead things, she spends time hiking, camping, running, and occasionally sitting down long enough to read. She may be found online at www.thegreenwolf.com, http://www.therioshamanism.com, and www.antlerrunes.com.*

Illustrator: Tim Foley

The Word as Gospel or the Road Less Traveled By?

Susan Pesznecker

We Pagan types think of ourselves as being quite clever and as taking a rather scholarly—or at least an informed—approach to Craft. I don't think it's generalizing to say that most of us have an insatiable desire to learn, study, and grow in our own practices. If one needs proof of this, just check out the volume of "Pagan" or Craft-related books and written materials that continues to grow with each passing year, each new book presenting a unique perspective and adding to available doctrine. Yet none of these books—so far as I've seen, anyway—has touched on the topic of how we read and study.

What do I mean by "how we read and study"? First and foremost, the question asks whether it's more important to try to decipher exactly what the author was trying to convey when she wrote the piece or whether it's more critical for the reader to be inspired by the piece, gleaning his own messages from deep within. Or both.

Let's imagine, for instance, that two people are studying a well-known text, like Raymond Buckland's Big Blue Book, a.k.a. *Buckland's Complete Book of Witchcraft*. Person A is intent on interpreting each detail of the text so as to understand exactly what Buckland means, including being aware of the time period when the book was written, the prevailing customs and beliefs of those times, and perhaps even Buckland's own background and experiences. Person A believes fervently that in order to understand and find value in the text, she must more or less see through Buckland's eyes, experiencing the material as he experienced it. It's almost as if she wants to be magickally transported back in time and able to talk and ask questions of Buckland as he pens each separate line. In short, she wants to get into the author's head.

Person B, on the other hand, might be mildly intrigued about Buckland's underlying intentions, but she finds more value in the meaning that she, herself, finds in the piece. Perhaps she's read several pages, finding it interesting but uninspiring; then suddenly, she reads a line and something clicks. She reads it again, and she's thinking, "Yeah…. Yeah." A connection is born, a click of recognition, a link to her own experiences. To Person B, it isn't that important to try and figure out exactly what Buckland intended in the past, but it's very important to find that point where the text touched, influenced, and spoke to her in the present.

Who's right?

I've heard people argue bitterly about these disparate approaches, and the discussion has touched many magickal movements, including Wicca and Druidism. In the modern Druid community, for instance, debate rages about whether it's more important to research, understand, and rely on the "authority" of the extant ancient texts or to read those texts with a focus on being moved by one's own interpretations and inspirations received via the words. Again, I ask, "Who's right?" Or, in the words of the immortal *Saturday Night Live*, are they both right? Is new "Shimmer" both a floor wax *and* a dessert topping?

As a college writing and literature teacher in "real life," I have these same discussions every day in terms of understanding literature, film, and other texts. I've been trained to examine writing, images, and other materials through a number of vantage points and a variety of critical lenses. I've learned to read both objectively and

subjectively, as a believer and as a doubter. The text is like a sphere that can be turned over in one's hands and examined from any number of perspectives. I'm comfortable with the fact that there's never an absolute "answer" regarding a text and that any number of potential answers are simultaneously possible.

Likewise, as a student of literature, I've been trained to understand that in the reader-writer relationship, there are at the very least two solid information streams. One has to do with what the writer intended when he or she created the piece, while the other has to do with what the reader understands or perceives when reading it. Both positions are equally valid. In fact, one can trot out the chicken-or-egg argument and suggest that without a reader to interact with the created content, the content itself would lack import. You know: If a tree falls in the forest and no one's there to hear it....

"Close reading" is a term familiar to literature students, and it could—and should—be familiar to students of magick as well. Close reading is based on a belief that in a text, each word choice, each sentence arrangement, each use of figurative language, each display of tone, etc., has not only been used intentionally but is key to the meaning of the piece. When one does a "close read," one reads with great care and great objectivity, focusing on each word, phrase,

sentence, and paragraph. Sometimes called explication, close reading operates on the belief that everything one needs to know about a text is right there in the text, and that with careful examination, the text itself will speak, offering up its secrets. In its purest form, close reading may not need a reader at all, for the meaning is already there, encoded in the text and not necessarily requiring anyone to ferret it out. I like to imagine close reading as holding a big magnifying lens up to the text, examining it carefully and trying to discover each of its secrets as well as how each part works together.

Those people who seek a magickal perspective directly from the text and its creator would be fans of close reading. One of my magickal friends, Rae du Soleil, is an alchemist in training, and when I discussed this idea of whether "Shimmer" was a floor wax, a dessert topping, or maybe both, she shared some interesting comments.

Earlier in the year, du Soleil had taken a self-guided class on interpreting alchemical imagery. She told me the class was "created by the man currently considered to be THE guy when it comes to interpreting alchemical imagery." His name [was] Adam McLean and he lived in Scotland. My friend noted, "McLean's point that he hammers home again and again in each lesson is that too many modern alchemists project onto the old images meanings and intentions that are beyond the knowledge base of the artist. His take is that you have to know who painted the image and when, and what that person knew and studied, if you are to truly be able to understand what alchemical information is being communicated with their art. For example, many people interpret a lot of alchemical images to have Kabbalistic symbolism to them, but McLean says if the artist who painted it didn't study the Kabbalah, then you're just projecting a false meaning onto the image and drawing an entirely wrong conclusion."

Du Soleil comments that most of the lessons kept repeating these points and suggested that if the student wasn't getting it, he or she should go back and start again. "It's sort of strange when you are doing a self-guided CD and get the distinct impression that your teacher is angry and yells at the class a lot ... but I got what he means, and given how the bulk of the alchemy community approaches images, I get why he's so frustratedly cranky."

Du Soleil noted that completing the course changed her approach to alchemical symbols and images. "His methodology has become a strong part of my practice now. I still take the time to look at images and think, 'What does that mean to me?' But since the point of alchemical paintings was to encode a person's secret knowledge and pass it on, I listen a lot harder to the artists."

I gleaned a number of points from her comments. If you're studying with a master, respect the master. Believe that he has something of value to tell you and try to keep yourself out of the mix. Consider the context, listen, and learn. But I gleaned points from McLean, too, who seemed to imply that to project one's own meanings into established symbolism was somehow a problem of ego. Or at least that's my personal interpretation (uh-oh) of his words. Returning to du Soleil, she seemed to reference her own frustration with the inconsistent way the alchemy community approached symbolic analysis. Her frustration with this left her relieved to find a mentor who stayed within the lines. The lines, in this case, were her friends.

Let's go back to the other view—that one's personal impression is what's most important. Interestingly, many of these folks still begin with original, historic, or elder texts, regarding these as the "real deal" and as seemingly more authoritative and magickal than modern texts. After all, the established works link to the past and speak with an authentic, deeply rooted voice. Upon reading those words, one may feel an instant connection with past generations and practitioners—a unique, intimate kind of access. But here's where group B diverges, because instead of settling in happily and focusing on a close read for the purpose of deciphering that ancient wisdom, these folks are looking for the light bulb moment—the moment of resonance. They're not reading to see what the master has to tell them: they're reading for themselves—for inspiration, discovery, and personal application.

Modern lingo has labeled this phenomenon "unverified (or unverifiable) personal gnosis," abbreviated as UPG. Simply put, this refers to that moment when the seeker has a private revelation or epiphany—a moment of sudden clarity or understanding. The term is attributed in print in Kaatryn MacMorgan's book *Wicca 333: Advanced Topics in Wiccan Belief* (iUniverse, 2003), but it probably popped up in casual discussion groups a decade or two earlier. Taken a step further, UPG can become CPG: "confirmed personal gnosis." This occurs when supportive evidence of UPG eventually surfaces, through direct confirmation or through textual support.

When people talk about UPG, it's usually in a slightly derisive tone. But is there anything wrong with this idea of personal epiphany? Isn't this why we read and study in the first place—to make discoveries and enlarge our personal spheres? To broaden our own little corner of the world?

Of course, this idea of personal revelation can, like any, be taken to extremes. For instance, some readers suggest the vulture approach to study: in working with a text, one should simply take what he wants and leave the rest. "Suck off the gravy and spit out the bones," one of my students said. Unfortunately, while plucking isolated ideas out of context and linking them together in whatever suits is simple, it inevitably creates confusion and leads to no academic good. In the most dramatic cases, this has resulted in spiritual traditions being built on the backs of spurious or non-existent information, as in the case of Iolo Morganwg. A Welsh man, Morganwg claimed to have discovered and translated a number of antique texts, many of which formed the basis for a resurgence of modern Druidism. Although it was later discovered that Morganwg had falsified many of the documents, people by then had become so enamored of his words and work that many continue to revere him today, arguing that even if his work was found to be falsified, his words rang so true that only divine inspiration could explain them.

And the beat goes on. Is it more important to read and value seminal texts according to the context and intent of the original creator? Or does the power of the individual play trump, finding what seems most significant and using it to move in a new direction? One could argue that any religion that remains frozen in place and doesn't continue to grow and evolve in tandem with cultural change is doomed to stagnate, and, potentially, to die. We could talk these ideas into the ground and never come to a conclusion, for we're humans, and we love to have our own opinions.

Ironically, the allegiance to trying to figure out what the author wants us to "get" supports the assertion that Pagans are big readers and search for wisdom through texts. Our habits suggest that we want the "Wicca 101" book, or at least we want it in our early days, when we're excited and want to know what to do and when and how to do it. It's a quick entry into the club. Perhaps then, once our thirst for new ideas and guidelines has been satisfied, we're ready to move on to phase two, the reading of texts with the intent of seeing how they inspire us, and where they take us next, and how they help us grow. The reader has, at that moment, reached a critical mass of life experience that allows the text to speak to him or to open his eyes in some new way. Is that such a bad thing?

Resources

Du Soleil, Rae. Personal Communication. August 30, 2011.

Susan Pesznecker *is a mother, writer, nurse, hearth Pagan, and Druid living in northwest Oregon. In her spare time, Sue is an organic gardener and herbalist who loves to read, take long walks with her wonder poodle, camp, play with rocks, and look up at the stars. Sue teaches green magick, nature studies, and writing in the online Grey School (www.greyschool .com) and is the author of three books:* Gargoyles (New Page), Crafting Magick with Pen and Ink (Llewellyn), *and* The Magickal Retreat: Making Time for Solitude, Intention, and Rejuvenation (Llewellyn, 2012). *You can contact Sue via Facebook or through her Web page (www .susanpesznecker.com).*

Illustrator: Kathleen Edwards

Witchcraft
Is Not My Religion

Tess Whitehurst

I know that words are just words: just symbols pointing at concepts for the purpose of communication. Still, words and their connotations have a tremendous amount of power. And I have to say that I'm not crazy about the word *religion* or the things I associate with it. While it can be necessary and appropriate at times, many of its uses have a stodgy vibe. What's more, it can often point to practices and concepts that are outmoded, violent, and even murderous. And, generally speaking, it doesn't feel particularly freeing or related to freedom in any way.

On the other hand, I do like the word *spirituality*. *Spirituality* feels like pure creativity. It points to our own unique ways of framing this mysterious experience of life so that it uplifts and inspires us, and so that we feel powerful, happy, beautiful, and free.

The way I differentiate between the terms, *religion* is a label used for classification purposes. *Spirituality* is an invisible yet delightful essence, like music or perfume. If *spirituality* is the infinite, spiraling, glittering cosmos, *religion* is a boring old book filled with crusty old ideas. If *religion* is a lock, *spirituality* is an open door. *Religion* divides. *Spirituality* unites.

Before I became classified as a "Pagan writer," I never really thought about it much, but now I notice people rallying under the label of "Pagan" or "Witch" in a way that feels religious to me rather than spiritual, perhaps by making statements about what constitutes "real" Paganism or witchcraft and what doesn't, or by alluding to the idea that Paganism/witchcraft is superior to (or even just in the same class with) "other" religions. And then I feel disappointed. Because, to me, the idea of witchcraft is that spirituality is most inspiring when it's multifaceted, kaleidoscopic, and utterly personal. In other words, it has nothing to do with being on any sort of team, doing things one way and not another way, or being for or against anyone else's way of doing things. It's a whole new paradigm that transcends those old "us against them" traps that have caused our species so much suffering for so many generations.

To be perfectly honest, I don't even consider witchcraft a "set of beliefs." The word *belief*, when coupled with religious-type ideas, feels both delusional and divisive. Spirituality is about reveling in the mystery and perceiving that which can never be truly described with words, so any one person's experience of God/Goddess/All That Is can't possibly be encapsulated in any one "set of beliefs." Besides, rather than a "belief system," I prefer to think of the magical

path as a dance of energy, a way of looking and listening deeply, and a method of being present in a way that feels fun, inspiring, and empowering.

But if I were to attempt a more straightforward definition, I would say that *witchcraft/Paganism* is a spirituality based on an awareness of the link between form and spirit, an awareness of our own divinity, and an awareness of the interconnectedness of all things. Seen this way, it not only has the potential to bring us healing and peace on the personal level, but it also has the potential to spread healing and peace throughout the planet. But in order for it to live up to all this potential, we must be true to it as a living, breathing, all-inclusive spirituality, and not as a stuffy old religion.

Living Our Spirituality
Rather Than Practicing Our Religion

One thing that I want to steer especially clear of is employing traditional practices and precepts purely out of habit or, worse, as a sort of prosthetic morality. To use two recognizable examples, some (not all!) adherents to Christian and Muslim religions appear to completely discount and suppress their own inner knowing and direct connection with the Divine in favor of what their church leaders say, or according to what it says in a very old, and often very violent, book. Because we, as Witches and Pagans, know that our inner knowing and direct connection with the Divine are what constitute our protection, conscience, and magical power, we must be careful that we don't fall into a similar trap. While there is of course nothing wrong with practices and rituals that inspire us and feel right to us, if we want to retain the fullness of our power and sovereignty, we must be sure that we are living our spirituality directly rather than practicing traditions just because they've become routine, or engaging in rituals or other practices (as part of a group or alone) that do not deeply resonate with us as individuals.

If we want to retain the fullness of our power and sovereignty, we must be sure that we are living our spirituality directly rather than practicing traditions just because they've become routine.

Looking at this from an energetic perspective, when a river is not flowing, it becomes murky and brackish and possibly fatal to drink. When a tree is not growing, it becomes brittle and dead. And when we are not expanding and evolving, we become stagnant, our life experience becomes hollow, and we may perhaps even take actions that are hurtful to ourselves or others. Our spirituality, as an extension of our consciousness and of the divine flow that underlies all things, must surge, grow, expand, and evolve if it is going to be vital, viable, helpful, and alive. In other words, staying in alignment with the Divine and staying awake to the magic of life means staying awake to what inspires us—personally and at this exact moment—not what inspired us yesterday or what a group tells us should inspire us or what inspired someone else years ago.

Letting Go of the "One Right Way" Trap

Many of us were raised in religions that taught us that there was only "one right way" and that any other spiritual paths were false at best and sinful or damning at worst. And I'd venture to say that—regardless of our family's religion or lack thereof—almost all of us were raised in a culture in which these "one right way" type of religions seemed to dominate the mainstream spiritual landscape. The big problem with this type of fear-based thinking is that it can innately give rise to conflict and even give people license to completely discount other people's intrinsic value and worth. Taken to the extreme, this is the dynamic that fuels many wars and hate crimes.

When I first began consciously walking the magical path, because I didn't know any other way, I remember naturally falling into this pattern without even realizing it. What I mean is, I just sort of assumed that by claiming I was a Witch, it meant that I was supposed to believe my way was the only right way and other ways were "false" or "evil" or "misguided."

The truth is, trying to figure out who's superior to whom (or who's right and who's wrong) is not only missing the point, it's also a total waste of time. While of course we're going to have thoughts and opinions about other people's beliefs and practices, we don't really know what each individual person is experiencing or not experiencing, or what precise path will be most beneficial to his or her most ideal unfolding. Not to mention, our opinions about what other people believe or practice has nothing whatsoever to do with our personal, direct experience of the Divine and our unique magical path.

Letting go of the "one right way" paradigm not only brings us peace and helps us focus on what's really important (i.e., love), but also, since everyone's consciousness is interconnected, it might be seen as the most powerful way that we can begin to shift the tide and heal the type of divisive religious thinking that has historically led to so much discord and violence.

Stepping Out of the Vicious Circle of Us Against Them

With the smear campaign that it seems so many religious groups and media outlets seem to want to continually launch against Witches and Pagans, it can be difficult to refrain from getting into the "us against them" action, if only at an internal level. Unfortunately, when we react with a desire to retaliate, or hold anger toward entire groups of people, we are less likely to further our cause and more likely to perpetuate the myth that we are worth fearing and condemning.

Let's look at this dynamic from an energetic perspective as well. When someone pushes and someone else pushes back, an ongoing tension ensues, both people stay on the same level, and no one wins. But when someone pushes and someone else steps out of the way, the pusher has nothing to push against, so he either stops pushing or falls; either way, the tension immediately dissipates.

Energetically speaking, I am proposing that we step out of the way by elevating ourselves out of conflict and into the divine consciousness, where all is one and all is love. (Because bickering is totally beside the point anyway, remember?) In other words, if we choose not to engage with people who may temporarily think they are "against" us and our spiritual path, we are embodying the solution rather than just perpetuating the problem.

To clarify, I like the idea of engaging in mutually respectful discussions for the purpose of both parties learning more about the other's spiritual orientation. As long as an interaction has this character, it can be wonderfully inclusive and enlightening, even if it appears to get heated at times. What I don't like or find to be useful in any way is the idea of supposedly spiritually themed backbiting or one-upmanship: interactions (on both physical and energetic levels) that are rooted in fundamental contempt or mistrust. When observing or engaging in discourses such as these, by taking just a moment to energetically tune in, it's easy to see that they always seem to exacerbate the tension rather than dissipate it.

We Have Nothing to Prove

While I recognize that there are times when it's appropriate and necessary to fight for our rights (for example, if we lost our job after we casually mentioned attending a Pagan Pride Day event), in most cases, it really doesn't matter what other people think of our spirituality. It's not their spirituality anyway. It's ours. So if they don't want to "legally recognize" it, or they don't understand it and consequently ridicule it, or if they decide to stop talking to us when they discover it, or just plain don't believe in it, I say, "So what?" We don't need approval from anyone else, and we certainly don't have anything to prove.

Julia Cameron, author of The Artist's Way series, says that "the first rule of magic is containment." One way we can practice this is by containing our magical inspiration in ways that nourish and nurture us, rather than weakening it by discussing it with people who aren't quite ready to understand or value it. I am not saying we should closet ourselves or be ashamed of who we are: I am all for speaking our truth, lovingly stating our beliefs, and having pride in our spirituality. I am just saying that spirituality is a direct, personal experience with the Divine, and that we don't want to cheapen it or lessen its impact by unnecessarily exposing it to the opinions of people who may want to demean or devalue it. What's more, it's important for us to remember that our spirituality is not an

ego-defining label or a rallying cry of "I'm this and you're that, and you'd better understand and respect me or else."

Besides, the most convincing and lasting way to gain the respect we crave is by walking our talk. This means acting with the knowledge that despite temporary illusions of discord, everyone is sacred, everything is sacred, and all of it is interwoven into one unified web of energy. From this perspective, we can see that rather than separating us from others, our spirituality unites us with them, and this is what allows us to do what we do best: infuse ourselves, our loved ones, and our entire planet with healing, blessings, and love.

Tess Whitehurst *is the author of* The Good Energy Book: Creating Harmony and Balance for Yourself and Your Home, Magical Housekeeping: Simple Charms and Practical Tips for Creating a Harmonious Home, *and* The Art of Bliss. *She's also an intuitive counselor, feng shui consultant, and columnist for* Witches and Pagans *magazine. Her website (www.tesswhitehurst.com) and e-newsletter (Good Energy) feature simple rituals, meditations, and musings for everyday magical living. Tess lives in Venice Beach, California, with two magical cats, one musical boyfriend, and a constant stream of visiting hummingbirds.*

Illustrator: Rik Olson

Pagans & Mental Health

Lupa

If you are applying to join Four Elements Coven, you must not be in treatment for any psychological or psychiatric problems or be taking any medications to treat these problems. The powerful rituals this coven performs work along similar lines as therapeutic practices, and there may be conflict with such treatments. Additionally, we can only accept people who are responsible adults and are able to handle their problems effectively, without medication or drama.

The above is a fictitious combination of statements that I have found in a number of online application guidelines on coven websites (which will remain unnamed). This is just one example of how people with mental illnesses face stigma in the Pagan community, though it is one of the more "official" examples. In my fifteen years in the Pagan community, I have seen a wide range of ways in which the mentally ill are discriminated against, from being barred from covens and even open rituals, to being subjected to Pagan community gossip and rumor mills.

Granted, this sort of behavior is sadly also reflected in society at large. Mental illness is still often misunderstood by the general populace, and even attitudes within the mental health treatment system can support stigmatization and other improper responses. While many Pagans may claim that as a group we are more accepting of differences than most people, unfortunately we still have a long way to go when it comes to reducing stigma against the mentally ill.

What Is Mental Illness?

Mental health comprises a whole host of psychological, emotional, spiritual, and even physical realms of experience. While in the past mental health issues were strictly compartmentalized, more modern approaches to mental health care take a more whole-person view. For example, old-school addictions treatment only looked at the addiction itself. Other issues, such as mental illnesses, criminality, and poverty, were ignored. It has only been in recent years that addictions treatment has taken into account the high rate of dual diagnosis—having both a substance dependence and another mental illness—in addicts, as well as factors that may contribute to addiction, such as a past history (or present experience) of trauma.

So in that context, what is mental illness? If you want to go strictly by the book, a mental illness is any disorder described in the Diagnostic and Statistical Manual (DSM-IV)*, the International Statistical Classification of Diseases and Related Health Problems (ICD-10, chapter V), or any of a number of other published psychiatric classification systems. Looking at the DSM-IV in particular, the categories range from disorders that generally start in childhood (such as autism or ADHD) to personality disorders (like borderline or narcissistic personality disorders) to mood disorders (such as the varying forms of anxiety and depression disorders) and a wide variety of other conditions.

However, for our purposes here, we can think of a mental illness as a psychological or behavioral disruption that significantly affects a person's ability to think, feel, or function in general society.

However, for our purposes here, we can think of a mental illness as a psychological or behavioral disruption that significantly affects a person's ability to think, feel, or function in general society, in ways that are not based in normal development or cultural norms. This is a very general definition, and I'm sure that (as with any similar definition) hairs could be split about it *ad infinitum*. But let it suffice for the purposes of this essay.

Anecdotally speaking, there are a number of mental illnesses that I have seen commonly in the Pagan community, though certainly not in a majority of Pagans. Various depression and anxiety disorders seem to come up the most often, though I have seen occasional people with psychotic disorders such as schizoaffective disorder or schizophrenia, and on rare occasion a full-blown personality

---

* The DSM-IV is due to be replaced by the DSM-5 in May 2013.

disorder. These have largely been based on people describing their own official diagnoses; while self-diagnosis may or may not be accurate, it's best to get a professional opinion just to be sure. And needless to say, it's not good practice for untrained people, even Pagans, to be going around trying to diagnose others!

Much more could be said about what mental illness is and how prevalent it is in both the Pagan community and society at large. If you would like to know more, please see the resources at the end of this essay.

Is It My Fault?

Now that we've established a basic understanding of mental illness, let's pick apart that fictional coven's mental health requirement a bit more, specifically "we can only accept people who are responsible adults and are able to handle their problems effectively without medication or drama." One of the biggest misunderstandings many people (including those with mental illnesses) have is that all you need to get better from a mental illness is to think positively, or at least think differently. In the United States in particular, the strong current of rugged individualism that shapes the overarching culture suggests that since a mental illness is supposedly all in the mind, a person who can't just "think themselves well" must be weak or flawed.

The reality is that it isn't that simple. Mental illnesses, to one degree or another, are caused by problems with the brain, either with irregular development of certain parts of the brain or imbalances in neurotransmitters and other chemicals. Some of them are hardwired in the brain (nature); others occur as a result of traumatic or other experiences (nurture). Each case is unique, just as each person is unique.

61

Despite numerous claims to the contrary, there is no empirically proven method for "willing" one's brain chemistry to change. So, for all intents and purposes, we can't just go in and flip a bunch of switches in our brains to make things better (though I'll talk more about medications and their effectiveness in a bit). Just as a person with cancer can't control the tumor with willpower, neither can a person with a mental illness just make it go away with the power of positive thinking.

What we do have more control over, to an extent, are the symptoms of mental illnesses. Numerous therapies exist to treat both general mental illnesses and specific conditions. Some of these are best done with the guided help of a mental health professional, though there are plenty of practices that a person may do in the course of their everyday lives. For example, basic self-care such as getting enough food, sleep, and time out from activities can help to significantly reduce the symptoms of a variety of mental illnesses.

What this all means is that mental illnesses are medical conditions and often are not quickly "fixed." Someone with a mental illness isn't deliberately trying to make everyone else's life more difficult, and no one says as a child "I want to grow up to have a debilitating form of craziness that makes it hard to have relationships, friends, or a job!" Additionally, the symptoms of many mental illnesses can directly interfere with treatment methods. A good example is bipolar disorder; during a manic phase, in which a person feels excessively energized, they may decide that they feel so good they don't need their medications anymore, nor do they need to go to therapy, which then can destabilize them further. And many people with depression experience such a profound lack of motivation to do much of anything that making the effort to seek out treatment can feel impossible.

Those who are generally mentally healthy often may not understand what it's like to be unable to function "normally." They may assume that the mentally ill are just trying to get attention, or are lazy, or creating drama. While people may vary in their consistency in treating their mental health issues, having a mental illness is not a sign of weakness any more than having a chronic physical illness means you didn't take care of yourself well enough.

About Those Meds ...

There is a great deal of debate, including within the mental health treatment community, about the role of medications in treating mental illnesses. Some people feel that they are over-prescribed, or that the side effects are too risky. Unfortunately, this has created a great mistrust of mental health drugs in general, and a lot of misunderstandings.

In my own experience as a mental health professional, there are definitely cases of people who benefit from drugs such as anti-depressants or antipsychotics. In my Master's-level internship, I worked at an inpatient addictions treatment facility where about ninety percent of the population also had a significant mental illness apart from their substance dependence issues. I commonly saw clients who had bipolar disorder, ADHD, psychotic disorders, and depression and anxiety, and there was a distinct improvement in their ability to function when they had the right combination of prescribed drugs. This was especially

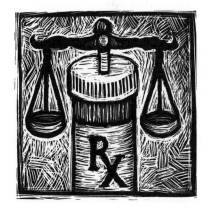

crucial to this population, in which so many people had turned to harmful street drugs to self-medicate illnesses that they often couldn't identify.

As with any medical treatment, the issue of psychiatric medications is a personal and individual one, and it is best discussed with a qualified mental health practitioner. With regard to Paganism and spiritual and magical practices, there is often the attitude that if you're on medications, you aren't going to be in the right mindset for spiritual or magical practices. However, if the drugs are successful in balancing a person's neurochemistry and reducing the symptoms of the mental illness, then they're going to be more present and focused than if they were untreated. The side effects of medications and the continued presence of mental illness symptoms, even if they are reduced rather than eliminated entirely, should be taken into account when engaging in ritual and meditative practices, but they should not be seen as an automatic barrier to spirituality.

Look at it this way: someone who is on medications is actively seeking treatment for what ails them. Isn't this better than someone who is untreated (and perhaps in denial) coming in claiming to be whole and healthy and then allowing the symptoms of their illness to affect not only themselves but everyone around them?

Spirituality and Counseling

And that brings up another misconception—the idea that you can't have an active spiritual practice if you're also in therapy. In my own training for my master's degree, I took courses on spirituality and counseling. Some of this was considering spirituality as a valid part of the whole person, and therefore just as important to the counseling process as knowing a person's family history or traumatic experiences. I also learned ways to determine when my ability to address a client's spirituality was beyond my level of competency, and solutions such as consulting with a leader in their spiritual community, making a referral, or simply directly asking the client more about their beliefs. We even discussed what to do when we had a client whose beliefs were significantly different from our own (and no, the possibilities didn't include "tell them they're wrong").

It is true that this is still a pretty new concept in mental health treatment. Many practitioners will avoid talking about religion entirely, feeling that it's more appropriate for the clients to discuss that topic with their own clergy. Others will talk about spirituality but may consider certain beliefs that differ from their own to be indicative of mental illness. Increasingly, though, literature and training available to mental health practitioners supports a diversity-based approach to clients of not only different spiritualities but different cultures, races, and other groups and identities.

This does require practitioners to be honest with themselves about personal biases, even if they aren't immediately apparent. And some professionals will be less diligent about this than others, which means that yes, there will be counselors, psychiatrists, and the like who will look at Pagan beliefs and judge them negatively.

However, if you are working with a Pagan-friendly professional, it is quite possible to coordinate therapy with one's own spiritual growth. What a good practitioner will do when working with a Pagan client (or a client of any other religion, or none at all) is not judge the

What a good practitioner will do when working with a Pagan client … is not judge the validity of the belief, but how the belief interacts with the person's ability to function in everyday life.

validity of the belief, but how the belief interacts with the person's ability to function in everyday life. There's a vast difference between "I believe there are fairies in my garden and sometimes I talk to them when I'm outside" and "I hear unidentified voices all the time that tell me to harm myself or others, and so I can't leave my home."

Reality Testing

Here's where we get into a lot of Pagans' fears about mental health treatment. Reality testing is measuring a person's ability to tell the difference between their internal, subjective thoughts and beliefs and the objective, external world around them. There are a lot of gray areas here, particularly when dealing with spiritual beliefs. For example, there's no way to prove that the fairies in the garden are any more objectively real than a schizophrenic's goading, taunting voices.

However, a person who simply believes in fairies will usually be able to provide a context for the belief in fairies (such as New Age spiritual concepts, Celtic or other mythologies, etc.), whereas the schizophrenic may have absolutely no idea where these voices came from, or might exhibit a highly paranoid reasoning for them. Additionally, a belief in fairies generally will not interfere with one's ability to hold a job, have healthy relationships (including people who don't believe in fairies), or be able to make everyday judgment calls that could affect the safety and stability of their life and those of others.

Most mental illnesses do not significantly affect reality testing. I have met a small number of Pagans whose grasp on reality is more tenuous than some, suggesting (though not at all diagnosing) that there may be some imbalance or illness going on. But this is not based on whether they believe in fairies, or even (like some Otherkin) that they are fairies themselves. Rather, they tend to have an inability to maintain healthy relationships of any sort (such as being very antagonistic without prompting, or being extremely shy and unable to leave their homes) regardless of what they believe, and this can make it difficult for them to interact with their spiritual community. Or if beliefs are involved, they tend to be wrapped up in other symptoms; for example, using spiritual beliefs as a framework for delusions of grandeur like "I have written ten books in the past year, each one on a different theory of magickal practice and disproving everything Aleister Crowley ever thought of; I just haven't found the right publisher yet."

Failing reality testing, in short, is not just a matter of having very uncommon beliefs. Rather it is more based on an ability to interact with the external world, regardless of beliefs.

A Call to End Discrimination

Interaction is the key. A big reason for mental health discrimination is that people simply don't know how to interact with someone with a mental illness. It can be unsettling, at the very least, to be around someone whose moods shift quickly and unpredictably, or who may say or do strange things. Often people respond by making assumptions about the illnesses and the people who live with them every day, including the misconceptions mentioned in this essay.

Yes, there are circumstances in which the symptoms of a (usually untreated) mental illness may become problematic; for example, a person being disruptive during rituals or continually causing conflict among group members. But as with any issue that arises in the community on a small or large scale, these need to be taken on an individual basis, not used as an excuse to preemptively bar anyone with a mental illness.

And that is at the heart of the discrimination discussed here: assuming that because a person is a part of a particular

demographic—in this case, mentally ill people—they will automatically behave in a specific way and therefore should not be extended the same opportunities as everyone else. Most of us would be horrified if a person in a wheelchair or who had to use an artificial voice box to speak were told that they couldn't join a group, or were subject to widespread gossip and ridicule, because they didn't have their "natural" physical capabilities.* Yet this is exactly the sort of discrimination that mentally ill Pagans often face both within and outside of the Pagan community.

How do we change this? First comes education. This essay is just one small attempt to educate people about mental illnesses, the people who live with them every day, and the challenges they may face

---

* Sadly, many Pagans with different physical capabilities have also reported discrimination even in the twenty-first century.

as a result. There are numerous other resources, including those created by mentally ill people themselves, dispelling myths and misconceptions while countering them with accurate information. The more you know, the more empowered you are to act.

Then there is compassion. You can know intellectually why a person is behaving in a particular way or why they are on a specific treatment regimen, with or without drugs. But unless you also have compassion for the person and accept that this is who they are in this moment, you may find yourself simply using the information to discriminate against them in a more sophisticated manner. Compassion isn't always easy, and having compassion for someone whom you may also feel very annoyed with or scared of can be even tougher. But compassion also requires you to come face to face with your own biases, and once you've begun to explore those, it becomes more difficult to uphold those biases and the emotions surrounding them.

Finally, there is action. If we feel that it is wrong to discriminate against someone else, then we are more likely to speak out against that discrimination. This step needs to be approached carefully; action isn't just the acts that we do but also the manner in which we do them. All the yelling and accusations of "BIGOT!" won't do any good if the person who is seen as being discriminatory is too busy defending themselves to listen to the message you're trying to communicate. And here a little compassion can also come in handy in trying to understand why a person may feel threatened or uncomfortable with someone who is mentally ill. Understanding someone doesn't mean you have to agree with them.

Even if you have a mental illness yourself, you can also make use of education, compassion, and action to stop discrimination. Your role may be different because you have the insider's view of mental illness, but being mentally ill doesn't mean that you have no power

Consider how you can change yourself and your thoughts and actions in the future; that's where it all begins.

to speak for yourself and others. If anything, your experience can be a powerful tool in advocacy, in educating others about what it's really like for you.

Consider this a starting point. Take time to think about what you've read here and what your thoughts and feelings are about it. Think about whether you've seen or experienced, or even enacted, discrimination against mentally ill Pagans. Then consider how you can change yourself and your thoughts and actions in the future; that's where it all begins. Before change can happen outside, it has to happen inside.

Conclusion

In a spiritual community where we often ask for help with healing, discrimination can make it difficult to request help with mental illnesses. Yet it is my hope that with time, there will be no more "guidelines" like the one at the beginning of this essay, and instead we may see something like this:

If you are applying for membership in Four Elements Coven, please be as open as you are comfortable with disclosing any illnesses or other medical conditions, mental or physical, that you may be undergoing treatment for. This will allow us to accommodate you to the best of our ability and seek out any necessary resources to help make you at home with us.

RESOURCES

The Mental Health Advocacy Coalition: http://02f1d31.netsolhost.com /joomla1

The National Alliance on Mental Illness: http://www.nami.org/

National Institute of Mental Health: http://www.nimh.nih.gov/index
.shtml

Pagan Therapy and Counseling for a Pagan World: http://www.Pagan
therapy.com/

Lupa's *complete bio appears on page 38.*

Illustrator: Bri Hermanson

Drumming the Dome

Paniteowl

Over the years there have been many stories told around campfires of people and events within the Pagan community; shared memories of good times, sad times, and times that will forever define who we are. This is one of those stories.

On Friday, October 13, 2000, a group of approximately 400 Pagans gathered in a grove alongside the Jefferson Memorial for the opening ritual of Blessed Be and Meet Me In DC (BBMMDC for short). The gathering was planned as a show of unity for Pagans all over the United States. The premise was simple:

show up and let others see you as part of the ever-growing community of people who embrace a wide variety of beliefs and practices. It was time to come out of the broom closet!

This was the third annual BBMMDC gathering, and it was a bit more organized than previous attempts. Workshops, social gatherings, and open "meet and greet" events were held at a hotel, but the most important functions would be the rituals performed throughout the weekend on the Mall in Washington, DC. The rituals were led by Wiccans, Druids, Heathens, and Pagans of varying beliefs. If you know the meaning of the term "herding cats," you'll know what an exhausting job it was for the organizers of this event, who were from various disciplines within our community. Working together was an exhilarating and at times frustrating experience for me, but one I will never forget. After a full year of planning, we were finally there, and magic was happening!

The opening ritual would begin at 9 p.m., but I was on-site much earlier, taking care of the mundane things necessary to accomplish our goals. Last-minute glitches were driving me to distraction, and we had to consider so many things. Most gatherings would have had a bonfire, but you can't do that on the Mall, so we had arranged for some portable lights, as well as battery-operated microphones so that the speakers and the leaders of the ritual could be heard. Well—you guessed it—the electronics never showed up. This was the year 2000, folks! We didn't all have cell phones to coordinate things, and that late in the day, we could find no replacements! OK ... not to panic ... we'd do without! We were Pagans! We would do this "Old School"—UNPLUGGED! Yeah, we were scrambling. Transporting people from the hotel to the ritual site was also a fiasco. We had given out directions for driving, and for using the Metro. However, we had neglected to check the timetables, and it was at the last minute we realized that the Metro wouldn't be operational by the time the ritual was finished. You could get there, but getting back to the hotel was a whole other problem. So we bribed and cajoled a LOT of people to agree to transport stranded Pagans. Again, we made it work, but it was hectic!

About an hour before the ritual was to start, I needed a break so I took a walk and wandered into the Jefferson Memorial. As I stood in the rotunda, reading the words of Jefferson, I was reminded of the reason I was participating. Powerful words that seemed to resonate in my heart gave me a feeling that everything would be all right. Of course I was carrying my bodhran (Celtic drum), so I softly played a few beats to ground and center myself. The acoustics were awesome, and I wished I could stay longer, but I had things to do, people to see, and a ritual to perform.

As I hurried back to the area of the Circle, I saw many people walking from the parking lot and along the sidewalks from the Metro. Flowing robes, sparkling jewelry, so many drums! These were my people, and we were going to have a magickal time. As I checked on those who really needed to be there—the speakers, the drummers, the ritual leaders—I had a chance to talk to Merlin, the leader of the Drum Circle, and I told him of my experience in the Jefferson dome. He smiled down at me and said, "Really!" (which is Merlin's typical response to people when they are blathering at him; I've heard that comment from him many times over the years). I thought no more about it as I was in a hurry to take my place in the center of the Circle as one of the priestesses leading the ritual.

A speaker's podium was set up at the edge of the Circle, where organizers of the event would explain the reasons for the gathering and take questions from the media. Meanwhile, the four of us who would lead the ritual began to ground and center and prepare ourselves to do the invocations when the time was right. I stood across from my good friend Reddeer and could see my own exhilaration

mirrored in his well-loved face. To my right stood Isaac Bonewitz, breathing deeply and gathering his energy to hold ritual space. Ellen Evert Hoffman stood to my left, quietly adding her energy to our small circle, preparing to open the gateways to encompass all who shared Circle with us that night. Two Druids, a Wiccan, and a Witch would blend their practices to create Sacred Space!

Finally, the speeches were finished and we were given the signal to begin the ritual. We cast the Circle, called the quarters, and invoked our deities. The familiar movements of working the energies calmed me, and the Circle became huge, yet at the same time seemed to be very close and intimate. Energy flowed between us in the center and then out to all who stood in this Sacred Space. There was no time, and there was no limitation. We were connected on every level of awareness: physical, emotional, and spiritual. Everything was in balance; everything was as it should be. Although we had no lights except for the full moon shining above, I could see every face, every movement, and hear every sound around us. Isaac asked me to open the gates, and I did so gladly. Leaving my place in the center, I began to walk the Circle, leading a chant of unity and joy. Merlin's drummers, I believe there were about forty of them, began to drum along with my chant, and the energy grew and swirled around all who stood in that Sacred Space. Three times around the Circle I danced and then reached out my hand to a friend, asking her to join me. She reached back and took hold of the hand of another in the circle, and the Spiral Dance began. I let the dancers go by me as I returned to the center of the Circle, reaching out for Reddeer, Isaac, and Ellen to hold the core of energy radiating around us. I have no idea how long the dance continued, but I found myself held tightly in the middle of the most rapturous dance ever done! Slowly, the dance ended, the drums drew quiet, and the ritual proceeded to its conclusion. We were done, we had accomplished our goals, and we knew the gathering would be successful. But it didn't end there!

The rotunda began to glow. People came from all over, seeing the light emanating from the Memorial. It was the light of pure energy and joy.

Remember I had told you about talking with Merlin? Well, it seems that Merlin told a few others about the "acoustics" of the dome. So immediately after the ritual, Merlin and a few friends (forty drummers and numerous others who had heard about their plans) took the opportunity to visit the Jefferson Memorial. It was late, the building was closing, and it's my understanding that the guards were in the process of doing their final rounds before locking up. The rotunda was filled with Pagans, and they began to drum. The rotunda began to glow. People came from all over, seeing the light emanating from the Memorial. It was the light of pure energy and joy. And people who weren't even aware of the ritual or the BBMMDC event were drawn to the site like moths to a flame! The drums were heard and felt for miles. I've heard many people comment over the years about the phenomenon of light emanating from both the ritual and the drumming in the dome. It was so extraordinary and gave many people an awareness of the energy we can gather and share when our minds and hearts are focused in unity.

As all good things must, this came to an end as the guards respectfully advised the drummers that this was not allowed and the building was closing. We had to leave. But it was all right, we had left our mark on that symbol of freedom and unity … we had

"drummed the dome"! As people quietly left the building, there was a young boy and his father standing on the steps of the Memorial, watching the parade of very satisfied Pagans. The little boy looked up at his father and asked, "What are they doing, Dad?" His father replied, "Making history, son." And that was the best comment I could ever hear about this event. It made all the effort, worry, and aggravation worth it, and it still brings tears to my eyes and a lump to my throat every time this story is told and retold.

The BBMMDC event was so very special to me and many others. I can't begin to list the names of people who helped to organize, or led the rituals, or gave workshops to give the Pagan community a wonderful experience. I also have to recognize the "mirror" events held by Pagans in other states, so that those who couldn't make the trip to DC could have an opportunity to share in the experience of unity. In the years that have followed, I've attended and supported many smaller events that got their start at the BBMMDC gathering. People who attended went home and organized their own groups to provide Sacred Spaces for people in their local communities. BBM-MDC met all my expectations and more!

Would we have continued the annual event? I believe so, but almost a year later, September 11, 2001, changed our world. It became impossible to organize an event in the DC area. The bombings of the Twin Towers in New York City, and the Capitol in DC, and the loss of the heroes who gave their lives aboard the plane in Pennsylvania were devastating and took something away from us as a country. It affected everyone directly and indirectly. But it is my fervent hope that we can once again have a Pagan Unity Event in DC, and that it occurs in my lifetime! I applaud and support all who continue to organize events and festivals for the Pagan community. May you all be blessed in your endeavors. I encourage everyone to attend, volunteer, and support these events, for we never know when something may happen that will cause us to lose future opportunities to come together. I look forward to the day when I can once again say, "Blessed Be and Meet Me in DC," or wherever you choose to gather—the important thing is to be together and build a safe community, a safe country, and a safe world.

There are more stories, and more magical happenings to share, but those are tales for another day.

Paniteowl, *simply known as Owl to many in the Pagan community, has been a familiar face at festivals and gatherings. Over the past two decades she has been a popular presenter, giving workshops and organizing events throughout the East Coast and Canada. Her articles and poetry have been featured in many periodicals and on Internet sites. She and her husband have a 56-acre woodlot in the mountains of northeast Pennsylvania, where they have hosted annual gatherings for Pagans twice a year for the past fifteen years. Owl also moderates a number of Internet groups, focusing on solitary practitioners, as well as Wicca Covened and Non-Wicca practitioners who want to keep in touch with the wider Pagan community.*

Illustrator: Christa Marquez

Witchy Living

DAY-BY-DAY WITCHCRAFT

Karma: East Meets West

Blake Octavian Blair

One of the commonalities between Western magickal traditions and Eastern spiritualities is a belief that whatever we put out energetically into the universe returns to us. In Neopaganism the concept is referred to by many titles such as the Threefold Law, the Law of Cause and Effect, and karma. The word *karma* has been adopted in the West from Eastern traditions such as Buddhism and Hinduism. However, the term karma came with alterations of the concept through attempts to assimilate it into our own personal and cultural beliefs.

Unfortunately, through these assimilations it has to some degree lost resemblance to the original concept. With the popularity today of blending Eastern paths with Western paths, it becomes important to explore the various version of concepts such as karma in relation to each other.

While the Neopagan concept of the Threefold Law and the Eastern concept of karma have much in common, they are not completely interchangeable. It is true that within both concepts what you put into the universe—on a physical, mental, and spiritual level—will return to you. This goes for both the "good" and the "bad." I put these two terms in quotations due to the fact that how they are viewed in relation to karma is one of the departure points between many of the Eastern and Western concepts of karma. In Hinduism and many schools of Buddhism, there is often far less focus on "good karma" or "bad karma" and more of an emphasis on "karma" and "not-karma," so to speak. Karma, when traced back to ancient texts, literally translates to mean "action." Action accrues karma. Although some concept of "good" and "bad" karma exists, the dichotomy between the two is not as prevalent. There is simply karma. Wise action, poor action, and indifferent action all creates karma. Simply put, in this perspective everything one does accrues karma. As with anything, though, there is some exception to this to be found. The religion of Jainism, which stemmed originally from Hinduism, has a stronger sense of "good" and "bad" karma. In fact, Jains believe that while harmful and wrong action accrues karma, right and good action accrues none at all. Without doubt this ties in with the motivations and practice of the Jain concept of *ahimsa* (nonviolence). Jain holy persons will go so far as to sweep the ground in front of them before they walk upon it so as to move any microscopic organisms that may possibly be in their path to be stepped upon and harmed.

The practice of vegetarianism among practitioners of many Eastern paths also holds ties to conceptions about the accruing (or rather the avoidance) of karma. The vegetarian connection with Eastern paths is also one of those more commonly drawn in the West in conversations regarding ethics and karma. With long traditions of ethics revolving around nonviolence, it is not surprising that many Eastern paths would consider the killing of animals for human consumption, when other viable options are available, to cause buildup of karma. However, it is important to note that despite common misconceptions in the West, the karma component is not the sole factor for practicing vegetarianism. Hinduism, for example, also considers the *gunas*, or qualities, of nature. Essentially, they feel that foods have specific energetic and metaphysical qualities to them. This of course is familiar territory for magickal folk—especially Kitchen Witches! Additionally for Hindus, while foods like vegetables and dairy products (the cow is sacred and thus so are dairy products) have the quality of purity, other foods like meat and liquor are seen as less pure and may provoke one to inappropriate action. Contrary to what many may believe, the majority of Hindus actually are not completely vegetarian. Vegetarianism is most common among the Brahmin (priestly) caste, as they feel the vegetarian diet is most conducive to cultivating a sense of spiritual contentedness due to the level of purity that they associate with it. The reasons cited by Easterners for abstaining from meat (and other specific foods) are rarely connected to physical health. However, physical health is a common reason today that Westerners adopt a vegetarian diet, in addition to spiritual reasons including karma and ethical reasons such as animal rights issues.

In the sacred Hindu texts called the *Upanishads*, karma is outlined as the correlation of punishments and rewards for one's actions. The question naturally arises of how severely will one pay

for karma they have accrued. The Neopagan "Threefold Law" supposedly denotes that your actions will energetically return back to you multiplied three times over. This is generally seen as a figure of speech rather than literally denoting a quantity or intensity. Another similar variation followed by many Witches and Neopagans is termed "the Law of Cause and Effect." This simply states that every action has a reaction, and many hold the belief that it will in addition be an equal and opposite reaction. In comparison it is important to note that Eastern concepts of karma make no particular uniform specification as to the intensity in which the cosmic ledger will see your actions return to you.

The next logical question at this point in the discussion is when do we pay for karma? … Depending on perspective, it can vary from moments to lifetimes.

The next logical question at this point in the discussion is when do we pay for karma? It is a cliché saying, "What goes around comes around"; however, it indeed does apply to the conversation we are exploring. The answer of course is not concrete. Depending on perspective, it can vary from moments to lifetimes. To begin answering this we need to address the Eastern concept of *samsara*. Samsara is the cycle of life, death, and rebirth. One spiritual goal in Hinduism and Buddhism is to be liberated from the cycle of samsara through eventual enlightenment, which generally takes numerous lifetimes. The Hindu *Upanishads* even go so far as to state that liberation from this cycle is the ultimate goal of all human beings. Likewise, an interesting goal in such Indic belief systems is to accrue as little karma as possible. This is a point that will certainly give the mind an intellectual workout, because as mentioned earlier, virtually everything has karma attached to it. In the East, the concept of karma is intimately connected to the concept of samsara. Your karma plays a key role in the number of these rebirths you experience, the conditions and types of lives you are born into, and connections you have to past lives lived. In essence, it is a cosmic merit system.

The samsara and reincarnation factors of the karma equation pose another large difference between popular Western views on the karmic process and those of Eastern belief systems. Popular Western concepts of this process often lack the long-term scope of the traditional Eastern perspective. The notion of "instant karma" is not an Indic conception. In Indic views, karma is worked through over multiple lifetimes. It is an extremely rare instance to hear discussion of karma returning and being worked through within a lifetime or less. Because you may well be working off or "paying" for karma accrued in a previous lifetime, it is also important to remember that you are paying for actions you have committed, even though you may not be cognizant in this life as to what these actions were or when you committed them. This provides great motivation to be conscious of your actions in this lifetime, as you never know in what or in how many lifetimes you will encounter the results! In contrast, popular Western karmic notions do provide for the swift return of karma not only in the current lifetime but sometimes in a matter of just days. Neopagan concepts such as the Threefold Law, the Law of Cause and Effect, and even the popular New Age concept of the Law of Attraction all leave provision for this swifter rate of karmic return.

The belief in some form of reincarnation held by a vast majority of Neopagans provides us with another commonality to Eastern thought. Of course there are some differences in perspective within

these beliefs. In Buddhism, karma is cited as the cause of reincarnation. Many Neopagan views do not directly place an attachment with or great focus on karma's factor in reincarnation and generally neither confirm nor deny its role in the process. Hindus commonly look to the devas (gods) for assistance in breaking free of karma and samsara, while Buddhists do not generally look to deities in quite the same way. The Buddhist perspective places more emphasis on personal action and responsibility. Both perspectives are similar to the practices and philosophies of many Neopagans for different reasons. The petitioning and worship of deities for guidance, assistance, or intercession in Hinduism is quite similar to the polytheistic practices of many Neopagans. On the other hand, the Buddhist course of action brings a great sense of responsibility for one's actions and self development. Responsibility for one's actions is known to be paramount in the ethics of a large portion of practitioners in the Neopagan movement.

When discussing reincarnation and past lives, it is pertinent to briefly discuss some of the different ways in which past lives can be viewed. When one breaks free from the linear view of time that tends to dominate mainstream Western culture today, a lot of conceptual possibilities open up. The predominating Eastern view of time is cyclical (and so is that of many indigenous peoples in the West). This allows for not only past and future lives but also for the concept of parallel lives. Many energy workers and magickally inclined people feel that because time is seen as cyclical, that past, present, and future are happening concurrently. Thus within this paradigm you can be (and you are) living lives in parallel. (This can be a bit of a mind-trip at first, I know!) Taking this view you could be working out karma from not only a past life, but also from a future one, because all are happening in the present in different realities or on different planes.

The idea of karma has permeated culture so deeply that it has also come into widespread usage on a secular level in pop culture. It has become part of our common vernacular. Yet the truth is that the concepts the term represent have been present in mainstream culture since long before the specific term itself came into popular usage in the West. The Golden Rule bears great resemblance to fundamental elements of the karmic conceptions we are exploring. The general concept can be stated as, "Do unto others as you would have them do unto you." Many people may not instantly connect this with karma; however, the statement does seem to implicate that one's actions through one form or another can return back to oneself. This concept too is in fact ancient and also has spiritual roots. A version of it appears as part of nearly all of the world's major religions, including Christianity, Judaism, Hinduism, Buddhism,

Islam, Confucianism, Taoism, and even Zoroastrianism. The relation of karma to factors like reincarnation, as well as the details of how and when one sees the return of their actions, varies from faith to faith, but the fundamental concept is there.

Karma does not apply only on an individual level either. Organizations, groups, and even nations can have karma. For example, if you belong to a coven it can be said that the coven as a unit has its own karma. All individuals who belong to the group are affected by the karma of that group. The same is true for an individual living in a city, state, or nation. The politics, exploits, and actions decided upon and carried out by the governing bodies affect the karma of its people. For me this serves as great motivation to be an active citizen and an informed voter!

It truly can seem as though for every answer we arrive at in our discussion of karma, we are encountered with another question. However, we can find a starting point by exploring these comparisons to establish a foundation for a basic framework of understanding. None of the views in this article are presented as being right or wrong. It is up to the individual spiritual practitioner to sort out their own stance and personal gnosis on the matter. I once attended a speech by a Tibetan Buddhist monk who said that in the eyes of the Buddha, we are the master of our own lives. In the context of this topic, I think that is sage advice! In today's modern world where the spiritual realms of East and West not only collide but also blend, we are certainly encountering karma face to face as individuals, a species, nations, and beyond.

RESOURCES

de Bary, William Theodore. *The Buddhist Tradition in India, China and Japan.* New York: Vintage Books, 1969 & 1972.

Embree, Ainslie T. *Sources of Indian Tradition, Second Edition, Volume 1: From the Beginning to 1800.* New York: Columbia University Press, 1988 .

Greer, John Michael. *The New Encyclopedia of the Occult.* St. Paul, MN: Llewellyn, 2003.

Grimassi, Raven. *Encyclopedia of Wicca & Witchcraft: 2nd Edition Revised & Expanded.* St. Paul, MN: Llewellyn, 2003.

Narayanan, Vasudha. *Hinduism.* New York: Oxford University Press, 2004.

Oxtoby, Willard G. *World Religions: Eastern Traditions, Second Edition.* Don Mills, ON: Oxford University Press, 2002.

Penczak, Christopher. *The Mystic Foundation: Understanding & Exploring the Magical Universe.* Woodbury, MN: Llewellyn, 2006.

Blake Octavian Blair (*Carrboro, NC*) *is an Eclectic IndoPagan Witch, psychic, tarot reader, freelance writer, Usui Reiki Master-Teacher, and a devotee of Lord Ganesha. He holds a degree in English and religion from the University of Florida. In his spare time he enjoys beading jewelry and knitting, and is an avid reader. Blake lives in the Piedmont region of North Carolina with his beloved husband, an aquarium full of fish, and an indoor jungle of houseplants. Visit him on the Web at www.blakeoctavian blair.com or write him at blake@blakeoctavianblair.com.*

Illustrator: Kathleen Edwards

Jingle Bells & Witches' Spells

James Kambos

As the year draws to a close, the holiday season comes upon us. Santas appear in every shopping mall and on every street corner. Holiday lights sparkle on lawns and in department store windows. And around the world the ritual of holiday cooking and baking begins to fill many homes with delightful scents.

Many faiths have major religious and cultural celebrations during December. There is Hanukkah, Yule, Christmas, and Kwanza. Most of us truly want to connect with the values and meanings that these December holidays focus on, such as family, peace, generosity, kindness, and sharing. But sometimes, the hectic pace of the season and trying to please family and friends can wear on our nerves and cause tempers to snap.

This can be an even stickier situation for the Witches and Pagans who gather with family and

However, even if you are a Pagan who doesn't observe Christmas, it's hard to avoid it. Most of us have family and friends we cherish who do celebrate Christmas, and we'll likely gather with them during the holidays at some point.

friends of other faiths. Some Witches don't observe the traditional Christmas season, but some do. Many of us were raised in Christian homes that naturally observed Christmas, so many of us still wish to celebrate Christmas—which is perfectly okay. However, even if you are a Pagan who doesn't observe Christmas, it's hard to avoid it. Most of us have family and friends we cherish who do celebrate Christmas, and we'll likely gather with them during the holidays at some point.

It's also possible that you may host Christian family or friends in your home during the holidays, and I'm sure you'll want everyone to feel comfortable.

The stress of holiday activities can double when Pagan and non-Pagans gather for the holiday festivities mainly because we both can forget about the similarities of our traditions. This can lead to feelings of "us against them," which can make most of us want to avoid family gatherings during a time of the year that should be warm and festive.

I've found it easier to be prepared in advance before a confrontation takes place. Unlike many folks, we Witches and Pagans have a few magical resources to draw upon to make any holiday season run a little smoother for us and the ones we love. So, my magical friend, while others are gritting their teeth, singing "Jingle Bells," and dashing madly through the snow with their "to do" lists, you'll be calm and ready to handle holiday stress with ease. You just need to prepare yourself both psychically and magically.

Since this is considered by many to be a magical time of year, I've found that a little magic performed now can work wonders. What follows are a few suggestions to make your holiday season a little more sane. Some are practical, some are magical, and most can be done without anyone knowing you've worked any magic at all. So, before you begin to deck those halls, begin to incorporate some of my ideas now and as needed throughout the season.

Daily Protection Magic

Begin each day with protection magic in the form of Words of Power accompanied with visualizations. This will help ground and center you. You may charge yourself and your living space with words such as: "There is one Power. The Power is perfect protection, and I am perfect manifestation of this Power."

Visualize anyone you wish to be protected as you speak your intention. Raise your power hand and turn clockwise. In your mind's eye see a white light radiating from your hand. See this light sealing your home within a protective aura.

Throughout the day, if you should encounter any negative situation or person, "see" that same light surrounding you. You'll be surprised how it will neutralize any negativity near you. This invisible barrier will protect you at a busy mall or as you're driving in a crowded parking lot. It will even keep you centered if the office Christmas party gets out of hand.

Any positive holiday magic must begin with you. These simple morning meditations will help you deal with holiday stress and provide a psychic shield. Let this be the basis for your holiday magic.

Crystal Magic

In many ways crystals are perfect for working some holiday magic. During this time of year when many regions are covered with snow and ice, crystals echo those natural formations with their shapes. Crystals are widely used by Witches and non-Witches for their healing and magical properties. This being the case, you can leave your crystals out and many will never know that they're working magic for you.

Use crystals you've already cleansed and have worked with for protection magic. Hold the crystal and respectfully ask that it send out peaceful and calm vibrations to all who enter your home. I have a large rose quartz crystal that I place in my living room when I need to create an atmosphere of peace and love. Most people think it's only a decorative accent.

If you're going out, you could wear or carry a faceted quartz crystal that you've consecrated for protection. It should help deflect any negativity directed at you.

For a beautiful and magical holiday centerpiece, surround your crystals with three white votive candles set in clear glass holders. Think or say "protection" as you light them. No one needs to know about their magical significance.

Holiday Candle & Fire Magic

The warmth and beauty created by candlelight or a blazing hearth are a part of both Christian and Pagan traditions at this time of year. Fire in any form—whether it's a candle's flame or a roaring fireplace—is cleansing.

To use candle magic to get rid of past hurts and mark a new beginning, light a red candle. As you light it, think "positive energy." To encourage harmony and abundance, light a green candle and think "peace" as you light it. A good candle to burn to purify and draw general good fortune is a bayberry-scented candle. Light a bayberry candle well in advance of expected guests and let it burn in a safe place. Bayberry candles are an excellent choice to use for holiday magic, especially on New Year's Eve.

A Pagan tradition that has been accepted by the "new religion," or Christianity, is the burning of a Yule log. The Yule log was usually burned on the eve of the Winter Solstice to honor the return of the sun's power. An oak or pine log was traditionally burned. Oak represented the God and strength; pine symbolized eternity. A more recent introduction is birch, which can represent the Goddess.

If you have a fireplace or woodstove, you can work some Yule magic by burning your own Yule log. This is a sacred holiday observance that non-Pagans will also appreciate, but you'll know the true significance of it. Select a log of your choice. Then tuck some dried holly among the kindling. The holly represents the past and old disagreements. Visualize past troubles being consumed by the flames. Here is another spellcrafting tip to remember about the Yule fire: If for some reason you're caught at this time in a tense situation, add some mistletoe—both the leaves and berries—to the fire. Mistletoe is an excellent all-purpose herb that can banish any negative vibrations, especially during the holidays.

To aid next year's holiday magic, save a bit of your Yule log and use it to kindle the Yule fire for the following year. To promote fertility, protection, and abundance for the upcoming year, save some ashes from the Yule fire and sprinkle them outside around your home and over your garden; this is usually done in the early spring.

A Time to Remember

The year wanes. December, our last month, walks softly into yesterday. The Winter Solstice passes and the great Wheel of the Year turns, and slowly—so slowly—  we climb toward another year, another spring. But as we look to the future, we turn to the past. Like our most ancient ancestors, we gather the evergreens to decorate our homes. For now it's time for "the hanging of the greens."

When the first people of our planet experienced the first

winter, they were in awe of the evergreens. The world was barren, but the great pines stood—silent, bold, and green. They were symbols of everlasting life. Even now, as each of us—Pagan, Witch, and Christian—decorate our homes with garlands, trees, and wreaths. We are not only reaching back into time, we are also reaching out to find hope and endurance. The beautiful evergreens of our winter world are rich with magical symbolism.

The pine, fir, and hemlock serve to remind us that there is such a thing as eternity. It is a common bond our religions share. Now is a time to remember that, although we may practice different faiths, many of our basic beliefs are the same.

Peace and good will to all.

James Kambos *is a student of folk magic traditions and customs. He enjoys learning about folk magic and how it's used in different cultures. He is a regular contributor to Llewellyn's annuals and makes his home in Ohio.*

Illustrator: Tim Foley

Magick for
Community Change

Courtney Weber

I live in New York City, in a neighborhood called Inwood, where grocery stores carry house blessing candles alongside Ajax and nearly every block has a botanica. Conversations on the streets are peppered with both blessings and curses. New York has forever changed my view of magick and the potential for its use. A few years ago, I had a conversation with a stranger on the street about one shop owner cursing another out of business. I laughed, but the woman shook her head and made an important point. "If that shop owner really had that power, why don't they curse away the drug dealers? Why don't they make an intention for clean air and a healthy river?"

I never saw that woman again, but I haven't forgotten what she said. It was true—why focus magick on small things only? I also looked to the religious communities of New York and how hard they were working to implement social programs to help the poor, fight pollution, and resist injustice. What could our coven do? We certainly did not have the resources of many other religions, but we did have magick. The purpose of magick is change—to manipulate and improve the circumstances of the immediate world. If the adage of "As Above, So Below" holds true, shouldn't Witches use magick for broader changes as well? Why not use magick to improve our neighborhoods and cities?

Before magick can enact change, the desire for that change must be identified. Our coven came together and discussed what areas of our city we wanted to help. In New York City, there is no shortage of areas in need, but we recognized that we had a large number of gay and lesbian individuals in our community who wanted nothing more than to simply marry the person they loved. We decided to use the magick of the traditionally marriage-focused holiday of Beltane to make such a rite possible for all people in our city.

First, we did our research. As it turned out, much of the New York government was already interested in legalizing marriage for all couples. The main obstacle was the State Senate. Typically our coven has invoked Pan at Beltane, but that year, instead of the typical "horny-goat debauchery" aspect, we invoked Pan's aspect of seduction: to seduce the sympathies of the New York State Senate. We set the altar with a pride flag, the State Senate seal, a quartz crystal charged during a recent eclipse, and a jar of honey. We invited guests from a variety of traditions and backgrounds including Minoan, Reclaiming, and Druidic traditions as well as Christians,

Yoruba, and individuals who did not identify with a specific spirituality. Attendees were students, housewives, seminarians, artists, high-level managers, and even federal government workers. We also invited an organizer of a Marriage Equality lobbying group, who spoke to us about the mission and ways to help. We sang, we danced, we pounded drums and shouted to Lady Wisdom and Lady Justice to "WAKE UP! WAKE UP! WAKE UP!" At the end, we threw our combined energies toward the New York State Senate seal, which was then stuffed into the jar of honey with the crystal. (The crystal was meant to open doors, the honey meant to sweeten the situation.) It was the most powerful ritual our coven ever had. In the weeks after the Sabbat, one by one, previously neutral or opposed State Senators announced their new support of the measure. That summer, in July 2011, marriage for same-sex couples became legal in the state of New York.

The true credit for this legislative success belongs to the activists, organizers, and organizations who worked for over a decade to make this happen. However, I do believe our magick provided a necessary and timely energetic push to make this measure a reality. Because of the right timing, attendants, and energy, our magick help invoke a change that bettered our community.

. . . .

When using magick for community change, make your cause specific. Are you in an area that is prone to violence? Do spellwork to increase peaceful mediation. Is poverty an issue? Consider binding rent hikes. Begin with research—discover what hinders your cause and build your spell from that. You do not need a large circle of people to make the magick work—it can be done solo. Consider placing a sigil or amulet representing the cause on your personal altar so it stays in your personal and magickal consciousness and make offerings to deities who might sympathize with your cause. On my altar, I kept the honey pot we'd created at Beltane surrounded by candles for Ladies Wisdom and Justice, which I burned nightly until the measure passed. Take time daily to visualize the change you wish to see and to remind the sigil or amulet of its job through lighting appropriately colored candles near it. These sorts of amulets can also be buried at places that need the support, e.g., a justice amulet at a courthouse or prosperity amulet at a school (remember to use nontoxic materials if burying amulets and make sure what you're doing will not get you arrested!).

Magick does not stop at the closing of the circle, nor does change happen solely at the altar. Consider allowing your gatherings to be platforms for community activists to share information. Volunteer for organizations that support your cause. If you're not sure where to start, pay attention to signs. When doing magick for community change, resources and opportunities to help the cause quickly reveal themselves through divination, omens, or synchronicity.

About the mechanics of this work: be sure to throw energy at offices, not individuals. Casting spells on individuals, particularly persons with great power, does not garner results. In addition, mentioning names of politicians in circle will almost assuredly invite snarky remarks from attendees who are not fans of the person. Snark will taint your magick and counter positive change. Focus on the role of the person in power as in, "We ask the office of the Governor to reverse its position on XYZ …" not "We ask Governor XYZ to do exactly what we say …" It's not the person you wish to change, but the policies of the government official.

Using magick for community change is not only important, but necessary. For change to happen, work must occur on all levels—physical and spiritual. These changes can happen through magick. Religions everywhere pray for a better world, and so can Witches. We just have a few more shiny tools. It's time to use them!

Courtney Weber *is a Priestess, writer, Tarot Advisor, performer, and activist originally from Portland, Oregon, now residing in New York City. She received ordination as a Priestess of Pan from Rev. Cyn DeFay of the Cluan-Feart Mystery School in 2005 and a Third Degree Initiation as a Priestess of Brid from Janet Farrar and Gavin Bone in 2009. She is the High Priestess of Novices of the Old Ways, a Progressive Wiccan community based in New York City and Portland, Oregon. She is the producer and designer of* Tarot of the Boroughs, *a contemporary, urban Tarot deck set in New York City with photography by George Courtney. She lives in Manhattan with her two cats, Lilith and Matilda. Stalk her daily habits at agirlcalledwoo.blogspot.com, @cocotarot on Twitter, or www.tarotofthe boroughs.com.*

Illustrator: Rik Olson

Pagan Home Birth

Chandra Alexandre

When I found out in April of 2009 that I was pregnant with my daughter, one of the first phone calls I made was to a midwifery practice to schedule a consultation for a home birth. Perhaps it was in part because my own birth had been traumatic and in part because of my Earth-centered, Goddess- and body-based beliefs; but there was no question in my mind (or body) about the rightness of having my baby come into this world in the most welcoming of spaces and ways. For me, that meant at home.

Of course, the medicalization of birth and normalization in the developed world of hospital births left many around me questioning my choice and fearful because of it. "What if something happens?" was a frequent opener from cautious friends and relatives. Assuring them that my attending midwives were also nurses and we would call an ambulance if necessary helped allay some fears. But the deeper, unspoken question for many was, "Why would she—or anyone—make that choice?"

In a place filled with the most innovative of technologies, state-of-the-art medical training, and painkillers by the handfuls, that I would choose a path traveled by most of the world's women yet uncommon nowadays in all but the poorest and most rural of communities in the United States seemed strange, to say the least, to many. To me, however, it felt empowering. It felt like the most right thing in the universe.

A most sacred act, an initiatory experience, and a consecration of love and commitment, childbirth is a culmination of many things, not the least of which are spiritual practice, intention, and faith. Within Pagan and Earth-based traditions, these components are worked through an appreciation of the profound mystery of life and connection to Spirit in the here and now of the flesh to underscore our beliefs. In combination, this and the fact of my own yearning to keep sanctity around all aspects of bringing my baby into this world were driving factors in my personal decision-making process. And while home birth is definitely not a possibility for everyone (there are myriad other factors to consider), it may be something you think about in a new way from this point forward—for yourself or perhaps with those around you in mind as they begin the journey themselves toward parenthood.

What follows are some offerings and suggestions for creating a home birth that celebrates all the joy, power, magic, and mystery of welcoming new life into this world.

1) Create your trusted circle. Your trusted circle helps to guide, protect, nurture, support, and hold you during pregnancy and throughout the time of your birthing. From the midwives, doulas, and doctors to the partner(s), family, and friends with whom you choose to share the forty or so weeks of pregnancy and ensuing post-partum time, you must know whom it is you can call upon with medical questions, for emotional support, to do ritual, to take walks in the park, or just as an ear to listen to your unfolding story. Having this circle ready will help create safety for you because you will know and trust everyone during the times when your faculties of mind are not easiest to reach. You will therefore be able to relax into your body without worry or concern. This will build a sense of ease into your actual home birthing experience.

From among this circle, you will likely select a few who will actually attend the birth. Make a careful choice, bringing people into this most intimate of places only if you truly wish them to be there. Then, as labor begins, you can draw these people to you psychically, doing so knowing that they will all later be physically close to help you through the experience no matter where you finally do give birth. They will be your champions and advocates, your soothers and energy holders, covering all parts of the spectrum of what you decide you need.

Finally, part of your trusted circle will also be those who are able to help care for you and those closest to you as you tend your baby in the days immediately following the birth. Arrange with them to have wholesome food brought by without expectation of a visit at this early stage. Also arrange with them to offer support for your immediate caregiver, be it your partner, husband, wife, mother, or

dearest friend, because this person will need another pair of hands. These arrangements will make the way easier for everyone.

2) Set your space. Create and cultivate inner peace as you walk the path into your home birth. This, of course, starts from the very beginning with awareness that all the energies you carry are being shared with your growing child. But as the birth approaches, begin by deciding where it is in your home that you wish to have your baby. Then, create a sacred intention for the birth while standing in that space. Once this is done, you may decide to dedicate an altar to the birthing and your baby; or you may wish to simply augment the décor with particular items.

For example, during my own pregnancy, as the weeks were getting on (and although I had initially thought I would create an elaborate altar), I decided in the end that all I wanted was music (I pre-selected songs for a birthing CD), candles, and two oils: one for birthing and one for healing. Everything else was perfect as it was. It felt special to me to honor as an altar the larger space of home that I had spent years creating. No matter what you decide, beginning to inhale and exhale the energy of what it is you wish to manifest and how you wish to do so into that space is most important. Visualize in that space so that you can manifest the coming together of your heart, mind, and spirit for birthing.

One final piece of setting my space was deciding what I would wear. I wanted comfortable clothes to start but, realizing that these would quickly fall away, I found myself one day taking all the jewelry charms I had from past covens, pilgrimages, meaningful family gifts, and magical work and creating a birthing necklace. I placed it around my neck when labor started, and it gave me strength as my daughter came into this world. Imbued with special memories and energy from holy sites, ancestors, spiritual teachers, powerful women, and others in my extended sacred circle, the necklace was a comfort. The sentiment of it now brings me incredible joy and reconnection to the greatest of mysteries when I wear it. Perhaps you will wish to do something similar, or you may be inspired to your own form of personal decoration.

3) Sustenance and nourishment. At the level of the physical, having a home birth means that your body is the lead voice when it comes to eating and drinking. Ensuring you are hydrated and have all the nutrients you need is essential. But sustenance and nourishment at the level of the subtle can mean that you have adequate means of tapping into the ready wisdom of your body, the depth of your intuition, and the sensitivity of your spirit.

For the first, your body will speak volumes in response to each undulating, rippling contraction, using the spaces in between as much as the pain itself to tell you what you need to do. Sustenance comes in trusting this information as the authority on what is happening in the moment. Supportive touch by your loved ones may offer nourishment to this process if it feels right to you, and constant internal check-ins with yourself will allow each cell to feel acknowledged. Honored by you in this way, the stream of information will keep coming. Use this input to increase your confidence and build a connection to your mother, grandmother, and birthing women everywhere.

For the second, intuition is the marriage of the body's wisdom with the faculties of mind. This occurs at the heart, the meeting place of downward-directed energies of the inner instruments of consciousness and upward-directed energies of the elements.

Intuition is the marriage of the body's wisdom with the faculties of mind. This occurs at the heart, the meeting place of downward-directed energies of the inner instruments of consciousness and upward-directed energies of the elements.

Reaching the depths of intuition means having taken the responsibility of getting informed on all aspects of birthing so that an undue amount of fear of the unknown does not creep into the process for you. It also means freeing your heart from any emotional turmoil so that it may open fully to the pouring forth of comingled streams of mind and body. Utilize your powers of intuition to tune in to the needs of your baby and the goings-on within your uterus and pelvic bowl.

Finally, for the third, your spirit harnesses intuition and presents it to the transcendent Divine, receiving a reflection of the truth that it conveys back through the vehicles of dreams, synchronicities, slips of the tongue, and similar outpourings. It does this to get your attention, creating a window for you to the fullness of your potential by being attuned to exactly what is perfect in and for the moment. It may also simply present you with instances of terrifying beauty and sublime wonder. Your spirit will therefore take exception to half-hearted utterances, acquiescences, and anything that does not empower you. Bring spirit alive by staying focused on yourself, in tune, and open to the will of the Divine.

4) Consecration and blessing. Blood. Salt water. Champagne. These three substances welcomed my daughter into the world. Anointed by each, she became part of the world of flesh, the world

of Gaia, and the world of inspirited community. As you plan for your home birth, you may wish to consider how you will welcome your child. After the initial time of bonding, cord cutting, placenta passing, and so on, will there be certain words spoken or rituals done? Who will lead and when is the right time to take this step as a family or community?

In preparing for my own home birth, for example, I took many walks along the ocean and knew that I wanted my connection to these waters of life to be part of this ceremony. As my time drew close, I collected ocean water and kept it refrigerated. When labor began, I placed it in the birthing room to be part of the event from start to finish. In this way, I felt that all the prayers I had uttered over the waves were present with me, and I could actively engage this element in support of my efforts.

Whatever you choose, know that the act of blessing your child in space and time cements your acceptance of them. For while certainly your heart and soul have made that clear, the outward act of ritual confirms and dances what is unspoken to the cosmos.

5) Honor and remembrance. Finally, you may choose to honor this birthday in a special way so that you can remember and share it with others. Certainly you can ask someone to take photographs or video or otherwise chronicle the event as it happens. But maybe, and interestingly, you will ask your midwife make a placenta print. These are magnificent, unique-as-a-fingerprint stamps of your and your baby's shared placenta that, regardless of mother and baby, look like a giant oak tree with deep, deep roots—a tree of life at the source of this particular life!

Another suggestion is to plant part of the umbilical cord with a sapling or seed that can grow with your child. A fruit tree may be a delicious choice so that you can eat of the tree in future years, teaching your child about the cycle of life as you do so. Whatever you choose, your thought and care now will give you, your family, and future generations much to cherish.

May your journey to home birth and the birthing itself be blessed and beauty filled.

Chandra Alexandre *is an initiated Tantrika. On her return from India in 1998, she founded SHARANYA (www.sharanya.org), a 501(c) (3) goddess temple dedicated to social justice through embodied spirituality and devotion to Kali. Chandra holds a Ph.D. in philosophy and religion, a D.Min., and an MBA. She is a home birth advocate and serves on the boards of several organizations dedicated to women and girls.*

Illustrator: Kathleen Edwards

Magick in the City

Melanie Marquis

Skyscrapers, asphalt, crowds, concrete—on the surface, the city landscape presents a challenging setting for magickal workings. Dig a little deeper, though, and you'll find the city is actually just right for certain types of spellwork. From magick on the go to spells cast using the city landscape itself, urban magick offers an arsenal of effective and practical techniques for the modern Witch. Our magick isn't meant to be limited to the circle, focused on the altar space—it's meant to meet the world head-on, and it can only do so when we use it often and everywhere. When you do so, you not only become more versatile in your spellcraft, but you also gain a deeper understanding of the fact that magick and Spirit can reside anywhere, even in the most unlikely places. Here are a few ideas to get you started on your way to becoming a true urban shaman.

Reconnecting the Vines Charm

Ever feel a little sorry for the trees and other plants that dot the sidewalks and streets, surrounded by hustle and bustle, contained in concrete planters and the like? Try this charm to reconnect city-bound plants to the whole of Nature, boosting the plant's power as well as your own. Show the world you are a caring and conscientious Witch, and the powers of Nature will be more likely to reciprocate in kind.

Place your hand on the plant and let your mind drift to wilder places beyond the city. Let your visualizations be enriched with psychic impressions; notice what stands out to you in your mental imagery of the more natural landscape, and pick a plant on which to focus. See the roots of the plant beneath the ground; sense the power flowing through the soil. Stretch this energy until it reaches the plant in front of you. Your hand on the plant, sense its energies and mentally tie this energy to the energy from the plant in your visualization. Imagine the energies fused together, bound by the common thread of Nature. Tell the plant that it is liberated, then leave some water or plant food at the base of the plant to set the charm and show your kindness.

One Good Turn Charm

Need a little good luck, a helping hand? Of course you do; we all do! Humans are essentially pack animals, living in communities,

sharing and trading resources, our energies intertwined. When we help each other, we help ourselves, not only by nurturing our shared humanity, but also by activating some good, reliable karma. Next time your fortunes could use a boost, go to the city with a pocketful of spare change and try this. Walk around as you contemplate what's going on in your life right now. Think about resources and opportunities you could use to help you achieve your goals, concentrating your thoughts on single concepts such as "money," "investors," "information," "friends," "a job"—whatever your specific need may be. Repeat this word as a mantra as you continue walking around the city, jingling the coins in your pocket. Keep your eyes open for parking meters that are expired or about to expire and place some of your charmed coins in each one you find. If you encounter a person asking for spare change, share some wealth from your magickal coin stash. If any coins are left at the end of your walk, leave them in conspicuous places where they will likely be discovered.

Mass Transit Magick

Many cities offer public transportation services, presenting the creative Witch with a unique opportunity to do a little spellcasting on the go. When you're in the driver's seat, you have to focus on the road and the traffic around you. If you let someone else do the driving, however, you're free to occupy your mind however you please without worry of causing a wreck. Performing magick while in motion produces specific effects that are optimal for certain types of spellwork. A spell cast while the Witch is in motion, literally moving forward through time and space, picks up the energy of action and movement, giving the magick extra speed, power, and momentum. This is ideal for spells intended to create swift change or to help you progress more quickly toward a goal. It can also be useful for magick meant to carry something away, be it an unpleasant neighbor you wish to relocate or an approaching misfortune you want to redirect and dispel.

First, create an object to encapsulate the intent behind your spell. The object can be as simple as a single leaf in tune with your aim, or as intricate as a carefully crafted poppet; it's up to you how much time, effort, and creativity you wish to put into it. To give an example, if your goal is to move more quickly toward furthering your education, you might choose a pencil as your spell object. To make it more powerful, you might bundle the pencil with a bit of St. John's wort or tie it to a piece of jade, adding any other herbs, stones, or symbols of the intellect and education that appeal to you. As another example, if you're wishing for a nasty co-worker to move on to other employment opportunities, you might use as the focal point of the magick an office memo written by this person, perhaps strengthening the symbolism by writing the person's name on the paper, or even taping a strand of the person's hair to it. What form the spell object takes doesn't matter, as long as it's an accurate and unified reflection of your magickal intent. Be creative and trust your abilities. Design an object that you think feels right—just make it on the small side so you can discreetly handle it on the bus or train without arousing "looks" from other riders!

Your object in hand and your intent in mind, catch a ride and let the spell be cast. If your spell is for bringing you swiftly toward a goal, imagine yourself and the energies of your spell hurtling forward, pushing you ever closer to what you want. When the ride ends, keep the spell object on your person or in your home until your goal is achieved. If your spell is instead to carry something away from you, envision while in transit this something traveling farther and farther away as the ride progresses. When you reach

your stop, leave the spell object at this new location, under a tree or in a planter, perhaps—anywhere you find bare dirt. If the spell object contains any non-biodegradable elements, put it in a trash can and bid farewell to the energies represented therein. The spell object should not be disassembled, or this particular magick will not work properly or as expected. Disassembling the spell object has a wide variety of other magickal applications, of course, as doing so scatters and disperses the energies encased within the symbolic item. The transit magick described here, however, operates on theories of directing and moving energy in ways that leaves these energies intact and unaltered, and scattering the components of the spell object would break down the magick.

Put some thought into the theories and principles behind spellcasting while in motion, and find your own best ways to make it work for you.

If your spell goal is to create major change or transformation, choose a transit route that requires a transfer. Envision your old way of being while on the first part of the route, then when you make the transfer and start heading in a different direction, visualize the new way of being you desire, the transformation you seek shining brightly just ahead. Once your ride is done, cast the spell object into water if it's biodegradable; if it isn't, hang it outside your home or in a window, in a place where it will be exposed to the wind.

Many variations of transit magick are possible; put some thought into the theories and principles behind spellcasting while in motion, and find your own best ways to make it work for you.

Be aware that using the subway to work such spells creates a different circumstance and symbolism, magickally speaking.

Spellcasting while underground is ideal for moving past old hurts or unpleasant ways of being, and it's also excellent if you wish to use underworld energies as an additional power source for the magick. If your goal is a regular, everyday desire that has few "dark" aspects, however, it is best to choose a mode of public transit that stays above ground.

Take It to the Streets

Now that you know some techniques of urban magick, try to formulate your own applications. The next time you find yourself in the concrete jungle, look around with a fresh perspective. Instead of finding ways to work around the lack of virgin wilderness, find ways to use it; ask yourself how you might make magickal use of the features unique to the city landscape. Might a public clock tower be of use in a spell to help you be at the right place at the right time? How about making a wishing potion with water from a public fountain? Could you use an elevator that goes up several stories for a spell to help you reach the top? How about creating a city sigil to help facilitate a move to a new metropolis? The possibilities and potentials are unlimited. Take your magick and your creativity to the streets, and the heart of the city will open.

Melanie Marquis *is a lifelong practitioner of magick, the founder of United Witches global coven, and the author of* Witch's Bag of Tricks *(Llewellyn). An eclectic folk Witch, mother, tarot reader, environmentalist, and folk artist, she enjoys a busy life enriched with personalized magick and practical spirituality. Visit her online at www.melaniemarquis.com or www.unitedwitches.org.*

Illustrator: Bri Hermanson

The Spirits of Place

Gede Parma

I am standing in place. When I cast the circle and weave my consciousness into the boundless infinity of life, I am reaffirming with every step, with every gesture, with every word, that I am occupying sacred space and particular place.

I am standing in place, and as I look out to the directions, I intone:

East of Here is Air...
North of Here is Earth...
West of Here is Water...
South of Here is Fire...

With each invocation, I am further aligned with place, and by holding this catalytic elemental alchemy within the circle, I am blurring both the specificity of place into the vastness of space and the current moment into the moving sea of time. I am also calling in the "corners of the cosmos" into the fullness of my own circle and remaking or igniting the cosmos by becoming its potent holy centre. In the living, limitless cosmos, there are no boundaries by which to mark a center, so to bring awareness to any being holding place within infinity is to magically and effectively become the center, thereby enabling oneself to hold the sacred balance and to weave with the wyrd directly.

However, for an incarnate being to hold center, we must be in immediate place and time—in the here and now. We must behold and acknowledge the living land that allows us to "start where we are" and have that be an explicitly and intrinsically sacred thing. It is the spirits of place that constitute the reality and vitality of where we exist.

The Significance of the Spirits of Place

The "spirits of place" are a broad category and in fact could refer to any point in the spectrum of spirits, if you will. For instance the river Ganges in India is considered to be the body of the Goddess Ganga, and therefore Ganga would be the spirit of the place of the Ganges. However, there are other spirits that swim within her body, and they are not necessarily discarnate beings or even deities.

As a Pagan I embrace my incarnation as flesh and blood as a direct embodiment and expression of my spiritual impetus and origin; in fact, I don't experience a dichotomy between either. I am as much body as I am Spirit because they are synonymous and the reason for one another—so entwined that I cannot see where one begins and the other ends. Therefore other spirits of place within the river

Ganges would include all water creatures, microbes, and plants; the spirits of the soil and earth in the banks that hold the channel of the carving river. A diverse ecosystem of spirits holds the vitality of the place and illuminates its secrets if only we would unshield our eye and looks directly into the heart of the matter—literally.

The spirits of the place are the native constituents of any region or area. They are the ancestors of the land; one day parts of my being will likely become spirits of place too. I say "parts" because I am a multifaceted being, as we all are, and there are modes or aspects of my consciousness and divinity complex which will not transition away from the living land, but become its immediate reality. My hair, my spit, my blood, my dead skin cells, my sperm—they will go into place and become interwoven into its wholeness; my personal vitality will blend with the overall signature of the place and add to and enhance the equation. It is because of this complex

combination of spirits that I will address the spirits of place using that somewhat ambiguous but all-encompassing term.

To acknowledge and honor the spirits of place is above all a polite act. Even though we cannot perceive four walls, a floor, and a ceiling when we enter "new" land, that does not mean that we have not entered a house of spirits. In fact consider the four directions as the four walls, the land the foundation, and the sky the roof. Further your understanding of this by the fact that the four directions are irrelevant and non-applicable unless we have a central reference point from which to judge our orientation—this means place.

If we do not honor and acknowledge the spirits of place in a location before working with deities and forces deriving from cultures and myths that grew forth from very different landscapes and people, we abuse the sovereignty of the land, of the air, of the sun that shines down upon it, and the water that nourishes and sustains it. The four elements are present in each place, and the majority of the contemporary Pagan traditions will pay credence to these raw forces of unfolding universe. Therefore why should we not also give blessing to the residents themselves who work with the elements to produce vitality that on all levels sustains the perpetuation of place. We would bring gifts—whether wine, food, or simply a kiss and embrace—to those we visit in their homes; why should we not extend the courtesy to the non-human? The non-human sphere encompasses much more than we could begin to comprehend. Our deities, many of them at least, are also included in this category.

Entering the House of the Spirits

Come to the place bearing gifts. I will usually bring spring water, frankincense granules, honey, or food (either specially made or broken off before partaken of) and a single white votive candle. I walk into the place and perform the following acts to enter into active recognition that I have now entered a house of spirits.

Breathe into stillness; consciously activate your/the holy center.

Perform a grounding and centering meditation; or triple soul alignment; or three realms alignment.

Face the east as the direction of the rising sun and look out to the farthest point and declare with pride and conviction:

East of Here is Air! Hail and welcome, Air.

Walk deosil (in the direction of the sun) and call the elements in the usual unfolding order (air, fire, water, earth). Simply substitute the direction and the element in the formula.

Return to the east and face into the center of the circle you have walked and sing with whatever tune comes to you:

In the Center of Here is Spirit—the Fifth that makes the Four one—I am held within your Mighty Providence. Bless me as I bless you.

Kneel at the center and light the candle to mark the fusion of the elements and the activated holy center of place.

Say aloud:

I stand alive and present within the House of the Spirits, and I have spoken to the East, the South, the West, and the North. I have knelt to the Providence of the Center and sung of Spirit. I am a child of Earth and Starry Heaven, and I come bearing gifts for the spirits of place.

Reveal your gifts and hold them within your hands as you channel cleansing and blessing force/light to charge the gifts for the spirits of place. When this is done, place the gifts around the votive candle and declare:

O Holy Spirits of Place—welcome me as I welcome you.

This is a way in which to introduce oneself to the spirits of place. It not only allows the making and offering of gifts to create a bridge of communication, a balance of exchange, but it also functions as an affirmation of place, a preparatory rite which can be used instead of a more formal ceremonial circle-casting. Indeed the circle of the directions has been walked.

House Spirits

The spirits of place are also definitely, for modern humans, spirits of the house, hearth, and home. Our houses are built directly on the land, and the raw materials used to form them derive from place. The foundation, the literal land and ground, upon which the house is built is sacrosanct within and for itself and also in relation to the fact that it supports the physical building enshrining the inhabitants. This goes for any building, even if you live in an apartment fifty stories from the ground; the building that you inhabit is still built either within or upon the open land. In fact, the land was undoubtedly scarred to accommodate the dwelling in which you live, and we pollute our immediate environments constantly and consistently with our house-cleaning products, rubbish and waste, artificial lighting and electricity, and the radiation that emits from our various appliances and conveniences. An offering of love and respect to the spirits of place in any given area would be to make conscientious and concerted efforts to minimize our impact upon the health of the ecosystem we find ourselves inhabiting, even if we live in densely urban areas.

- Replace house-cleaning products with environmentally sound, naturally derived, organic, and nontoxic products. Do this also for all health, beauty, and hygiene products as much as possible. Consider the impact commercially sold vitamins have on the waterways—replace with organic food sources rich in active vitamins and nutrients.

- Minimize pre-packaged, plastic-wrapped food products and recycle everything and anything possible. Learn the regional rules and regulations for recycling and follow them strictly to encourage and aid the process. DO NOT litter; this includes the butts of cigarettes if you are a smoker.

- Replace all light bulbs in the house/apartment with energy-efficient light bulbs if electricity is the power source. Consider switching to a carbon-neutral program with your power provider or connecting to solar or wind-powered systems.

- Minimize the use of microwaves altogether or donate it to a second-hand/bargain store. Purchase or change to energy-efficient white appliances, especially refrigerators; consider limiting the household to only one refrigerator if possible.

- Turn off artificial lighting when leaving rooms and consider soy-based or beeswax candles for natural, ambient lighting (remember fire safety!).

- Reject bottled water and invest in a water filter or, if the taste of tap-water revolts you and feels wrong, purchase spring water from reputable and eco-friendly companies who recycle their containers.

- Buy furniture and clothes from second-hand stores or reputable, eco-friendly/organic companies and lines/designers.

- Eat locally-grown and organic food.

These are highly significant and engaged acts that should not just be practiced by devoted Earth-reverent Pagans, but by anyone living upon Earth. They are offerings of the utmost attention and compassion. The sacred balance and exchange is formed, and if each of these acts is approached with the correctly aligned attitude, the energy raised will be as potent as any ritualized spell.

On a more "esoteric" level, house spirits are usually very talkative, and unless a devastating or traumatic event or series of abuses occurred to the particular being or generally within the house, the imprint should be far more neutral. However, a good home should have immediate character. To communicate with the spirits of the house, simply start talking aloud as you move around and through the dwelling. Explain your intentions, especially if you are about to embark on a cleansing and blessing of the residence (which you should). Make it explicitly known that your ritual intends to cleanse

stagnant life-force energy and to open a flow of vitality through the home that will banish all malevolence (if any exists/persists) and create boundaries of protection to guard the home and those within it. As you carry out your conversations and your ritual of home blessing, you will gradually receive the stories and impressions of the resident spirits. In my most recent move, during the last phase of my house blessing and protection work, I met with the spirit of place who exists in the very soil that supports my house. I consider "him" the house spirit now, and because I first perceived him as a nebulous pink shining light within the soil, I created an energetic home for him within a chunk of rose quartz that sits in the central room of the house (the living room, in this case).

Rejoicing with the Spirits of Place

Too often in contemporary traditions of magick and Witchcraft we forget to simply let go and enjoy the moment—and the place! We forget that indulging does not necessarily have to affect our health in any negative or debilitating way, but it can actually enhance and deepen it on all levels and in every aspect, not just physically. One of the best examples to convey this truth is the Faerie March of the WildWood Tradition in Brisbane City, Australia, on Beltane—the Feast of Love. In the Southern Hemisphere, this occurs in the beginning of November.

In the middle of the day we gather in Victoria Park in the centre of the city. A stern-looking statue of Queen Victoria gazes over the green square flanked by the river, the casino, and government offices. We come dressed as the wild denizens of Fey—as the primal spirits of place—and we sing, dance, blow bubbles, and sprinkle the sacred ground with petals of proud summer-hopeful blossoms. We sing, chant, drum, and dance and connect with the living land and the sky above. We then form a procession and move through the city awakening the Earth in the concrete jungle and arousing smiles from every passerby. We sing and we carry the Faerie Bull, who is full of sweets and candy. We will sacrifice him at the ceremony on the hill in Roma St. Parklands after we cast the circle, honor the elements and acknowledge our sacred four. He offers forth his sweet bounty and we partake in relish and revel. Our Lady of the Moon, Queen of the Faeries, and our Stag-Horned God who at the equinox was crowned as King of the Light are welcomed in embodied form within the vessels of Witches. Later, after the sun has set, our family, the Wildkin, gathers and continues to celebrate in wild abandon.

The spirits spin and dance with us as we kiss, touch, and ignite the sensuality of this sacred festival. They smile, shriek, and laugh with us as we drink, eat, and make merry with red roses, full of the zest of life.

Gede Parma is a Witch, Pagan Mystic, initiated Priest, and award-winning author. He is an initiate and teacher of the WildWood Tradition of Witchcraft, a hereditary healer and seer with Balinese-Celtic ancestry, and an enthusiastic writer and author of Ecstatic Witchcraft, Spirited, and By Land, Sky & Sea. Gede is a proactive and dynamic teacher and is also the creator and facilitator of the two-year Shamanic Craft Apprenticeship. He teaches mainly in Australia, but has also taught in the United States, United Kingdom, and Ireland. Gede was a speaker at the 2009 Parliament of the World's Religions and at Auburn Theological Seminary in New York City. Gede is the devoted priest of Persephone, Hekate, Hermes, Aphrodite, and the Sacred Four of the WildWood. His spiritual path is highly syncretic and incorporates elements of traditional shamanisms, Balinese Hinduism, British-Celtic Witchcraft, Stregheria, Greek Paganism, Feri, Reclaiming, and WildWood Witchcraft. You can visit Gede at www.gedeparma.com.

Illustrator: Christa Marquez

Integrating the Energies of North and South

Marye-Ann Azzarello

As the Wheel of the Year turns, Pagans are very aware of the daily subtle shift in the temperatures and energies that signal a move toward the new season. If you have ever taken a trip from one hemisphere to the other at the time of a holy day, you'll have an idea of what I mean.

I am an ex-pat American now resident in Australia for nearly twenty years, and I still well remember my first Samhain in the south. I had arrived in Queensland on October 23, and by October 31, I was ready for the new year knowing that my coven in California was celebrating Samhain while the secular world celebrated Halloween. In those days Australia, while not yet into Halloween in quite the same way as America, was nonetheless beginning to give a nod to ghosts and Witches on the day. The oddity for me was the very noticeable difference in the overall energies around me. As the Global Deep South prepared to celebrate "Halloween," it was apparent that the feel in the air was of Beltane and spring. Not only were the temperatures proclaiming it to be spring, but the buzz in the air that is the "feel" of energy was all about newness and beginnings.

When Samhain Is Not Halloween

Since non-Pagans were not celebrating a holy day but rather a secular fun day full of costumes and trick or treat, the general public was not concerned with how the atmosphere felt, but it was certainly noticeable to me, as it would be to any Pagan who is energy conscious.

I made it through the pretense that October 31 was Samhain, but by the time December 21 in sub-tropical Queensland came around, I began to realize there was no way I could pretend it was the Winter Solstice, even if the shops were touting Yule as Christmas. Again the physical temperature made this apparent, as the thermometers hit the 90s and then added humidity as an extra. However, as with my experience on October 31, I could feel that the energy buzz was definitely not saying "midwinter." Like it or not, it was clearly summertime.

I nonetheless made the attempt to organize Yule on the date I was used to, but after a distinctly unsuccessful try to arrange the Winter Solstice in December (with that pesky thermometer registering in the high 90s and on up to 100 degrees F on most days), I set about celebrating Litha, the Summer Solstice.

Summer in Winter

But I found myself again experiencing a strange disoriented feeling. It was odd knowing that my fellow Pagans in our California group were getting ready to welcome the return of the Sun as the Wheel of the Year once more moved round.

I organized the Summer Solstice altar using the local fruits and flowers of the season, which included tropical offerings such as plumeria and papaya. I had previously lived many years in Hawaii, raising my three sons there. I thus have a deep affinity and love for the fiftieth state, so the tropics and the tropical foliage struck a happy chord. However, there was still that nagging thought about what my West Coast Pagan friends were doing, and it didn't include tropical fruits and blossoms.

I began to focus my attention on the energies of the Northern Hemisphere. I placed a red candle with some evergreen branches on a corner of my altar, then added a handful of nuts in their shells. I sat and contemplated this small area of Winter Solstice energy, and slowly I began to feel it.

From this initial beginning was born my eventual understanding that the circling energies that move around Mother Earth can be felt wherever we are, if we only focus our awareness and pay attention. To this end I began experimenting with ways to draw in the various energies and feel them in combination, while still noticing their individuality.

Color, Scent, and the Elements

I started with one of my favorite magical practices: the combined use of color and scent, with the energies of the different elements. I have always been very interested in candle magic—that wonderful mixture of the energy of fire together with the earth energy of the

candle itself. When we add the energy of the candle's color, and it's scent (if applicable), we have very potent magic in a very small package. It was therefore with candle magic that I began my search for ways to bring the northern and southern energies together.

A first step (and one that I suggest if you wish to try this) is to place upon the holy day altar a candle that is representative of the other side of Earth. To a Samhain altar where you may have black and orange candles, a jack-o-lantern, and perhaps a representation of Hekate the Crone Mother, we can add a small piece of spring. On a corner of the altar place a soft yellow candle surrounded by spring flowers. These can be paper, silk, or plastic if nothing fresh is available. What we are doing is making a focal point for our attention to become aware of what is happening on the other side of our world.

As we in the south celebrate Samhain, the beginning of the new year, we become cognizant of the fact that in the north our Pagan brothers and sisters are celebrating Beltane, which is also a festival of newness and the beginnings associated with fertility.

By focusing attention on these two holy days and their meanings, we will begin to get a sense of all of the energies—those in which we are living and those in the opposite half of our world. By simply noticing we begin to feel.

Each holy day that we celebrate has an opposite that is being celebrated at the same time of year on the other side of Earth. Imbolc is a feast of light, while Lammas draws our attention to the approaching darkness. Ostara and Mabon celebrate the vernal and autumnal equinoxes, at the same time but in a different place. Both of these holidays occur when the number of hours of daylight and darkness are the same, though in the one case the light is becoming stronger while in the other it is weakening. We now come to the solstices—Yule in the winter and Litha in the summer—commemorating the longest and the shortest nights of the year. Again this is a reminder of how the sun's light comes to us in different ways.

As we look at a listing of our special days from this different point of view, we can see the similarities and realize that perhaps the biggest single difference is in the outside temperature. From the cold of Yule to the heat of Litha; from the chill of Samhain to the warmth of Beltane, and so on.

Now armed with this specialized knowledge, we can begin to focus our hearts and our thoughts on the feel of the energy. The first thing we will notice is the energy where we actually are. At Yule certainly the temperature of the air is different than that of Litha, but also the energy itself is different. There is a feeling of movement on both days, with Yule gently shifting toward the sunlight while Litha, in the midst of summer's heat, makes the same gentle shift away, beginning the move toward winter. We understand how each day following the Solstice means that the sunlight is either growing a little stronger or a little weaker, depending on where we are. Now we take note of that same but opposite feeling that is occurring at this same time on the other side of Mother Earth.

As you work with this concept you begin to get a feeling of total connectedness—with all parts of our Earth and with Pagans everywhere. We understand that while we celebrate the new year ener-gies of Samhain, on our Earth's opposite side Pagans are celebrating the newness of spring. The new year of Samhain leads us toward winter and the quiet time of introspection when we can plan new projects and nurture new ideas. The central spring newness of Beltane leads us toward fruition and fertility and the bounty of harvest, which will include harvesting the bounty of projects planned during the dark and quiet months.

We find as we make a point of feeling all of the energies of the Earth that our ritual practices and our spellcrafting become much more meaningful. We have removed the limitations of only one season and allowed ourselves to be a part of the whole, experiencing both the whole Earth and the whole Wheel of the Year.

It takes some practice to feel those opposite energies, but with thought and concentration, it will happen. I perfected the technique by spending some time each week focusing totally on the energies of the opposite side of Earth. I was not working with holy day energy but rather with the everyday feel of place. I would note the date on the calendar—let's say July 10. Living in Australia's tropical Queensland this didn't mean snow and ice, but it was midwinter and it felt like it. I would dress warmly and sit in the sun. Focusing on the warmth rather than the date or the season, I then turned my thoughts toward the Northern Hemisphere. I closed my eyes and brought up pictures of my former home in the San Jose area of California. I saw myself there in the midsummer of

It takes some practice to feel those opposite energies but with thought and concentration, it will happen.

July. I reminded myself that the same sun was shining on me here in Queensland, only the sun's heat would be greater in July in California because the world was turning.

Bringing up a series of mental pictures of the summertime July of California, I then revisited a Summer Solstice ritual. By mentally moving through that ritual, seeing the fight between the Oak King and the Holly King when the Oak King dies, I felt an actual change in the energy. Not just the temperatures around me, but the energies within me. And at last I felt myself experiencing both hemispheres, and the energies of north and south were combined for me.

Spellcasting Worldwide

Think about spellwork in this context as an example. If you have an ailing friend and are working a health spell, consider using both north and south energies. If it's summer where you are, focus the energy on the glorious growth of summer and see your friend glowing with warmth and bountiful health. With that picture and feeling in your mind and heart, next focus on the peaceful slowing down of winter that is happening in the opposite hemisphere and see the illness also slowing down and diminishing, allowing calm and peace to return.

If money is needed and you are working a prosperity spell, again see (and do your best to feel) the summer energies growing and burgeoning with life, bringing in a harvest of whatever is required to meet your needs. Simultaneously see and feel the energies of winter calming and quieting your money worries. Feel the peace of a gentle winter scene all around you, perhaps a winter fireside in a quiet hunting lodge, or a country kitchen in winter with apples stewing on the stove.

To help you get the feel of those opposite energies, you can use such things as fresh herbs from the supermarket to give a summer feel to your wintertime altar. If it is summer where you are, then give the feel of winter with a small dish of crushed ice with a floating candle on it. As the ice melts, the candle floats, and this change too helps us to feel a shift in energy.

When you are working in this way, you can kick-start the process by getting a clear picture in your mind's eye of a scene where you live that is appropriate to what you are looking toward. When you have that firmly in place, move on to creating a similar appropriate picture using the feel of the opposite season. One good way to get used to this is to see yourself in a place where you have been at various times of the year. Perhaps a nearby beach where you swim in the summer and bundle up warmly to take a brisk walk in the winter. The place is the same, but the energy of the seasons will be different. In the same way, as we move from one side of Earth to the other, the place will now be different but the energy of the seasons will be the same.

With modern travel this happens quickly. Board a plane in San Francisco in December and it is wintertime; when you land in Sydney and disembark, it is very noticeably summer. The first clue is the temperature—and that's a clue you can't miss! Next, as you tune in to the energy, you feel that additional shift, and you are one with the whole world.

For many years now I have been celebrating the Summer Solstice here in Australia in December with a beautiful and fun-filled open ritual on the beach. The Oak King and the Holly King fight—often with pool noodles and much laughter. We cast the circle by having the older children race around the edges with sparklers and everyone claps and chants "the circle is cast!" We are often joined by non-Pagans who come to see just what we're up to and to add some "Christmas cheer" to the festivities. In the midst of the fun and hilarity, the feel of total connectedness with Mother Earth and people everywhere is very strong. Peace on Earth at last feels like a real possibility.

Marye-Ann Azzarello is an ex-pat American and a retired lawyer who has lived in Australia now for nearly twenty years. She is the elder Crone in the Earthwyrm Coven in Queensland, where she also teaches the Craft and metaphysical studies. Marye-Ann has been a feature writer for White Light (an Australian quarterly magazine) for many years and was a contributor to Crafting the Community, an anthology of personal stories from the Australian Pagan community. You can reach her at maryeann .azzarello@gmail.com.

Illustrator: Kathleen Edwards

Witchcraft Essentials

PRACTICES, RITUALS & SPELLS

Dark Moon Break

Denise Dumars

We all need a break sometimes, and it seems as if our busy lives hardly allow us any. The importance of this topic really came home to me when I was talking to my hairdresser—one of the hardest-working people I know—and she told me that she was actually looking forward to attending traffic school on a Saturday because it would force her to sit down and be quiet for a day! Do you know anyone like that? I found her entire situation cosmically symbolic: her speeding ticket was a message to slow down in more than one way, evidently.

Most of us have to schedule our down time, something our grandparents (well, my grandparents; maybe your great-great-grandparents) would laugh at. Labor leaders sacrificed a lot—sometimes even their own lives—to bring us a forty-hour work week and two days off, and what a tragedy it is that this schedule is no longer the norm for most working people. Then there are the people who "don't work"—you know, those women we think are "just homemakers" and those men we call "stay-at-home dads." They have the hardest jobs of all, I think. Finally, there are the students—high school students seem to have every hour of every day scheduled for them in some way or another, which can't be much fun. We all need free, unstructured time in our lives.

So for all the hardworking people out there, regardless of what your "job" is, the time of the dark moon/new moon is traditionally considered fallow time, time to rest. And if we schedule everything else in our lives, then we should definitely schedule a time to rest and recharge.

While there is some disagreement about whether the dark moon and the new moon are the same thing—some say the dark moon precedes the new moon—whatever the case, the new moon will be marked on your Llewellyn calendar as well

So for all the hardworking people out there, regardless of what your "job" is, the time of the dark moon/new moon is traditionally considered fallow time, time to rest.

as others. This lunar event marks the between-time, the time when the mystical world seems suspended in time, when neither action nor reaction seem appropriate on the magical level. Once the moon begins to wax, then we can become magically active again, so why not use the dark moon as a way to take a break from your mundane life activities as well as from your magical activities?

So this break's for you, Bud (Bud in hand or not!). There are two versions: the long and the short, and both should be "scheduled" at the time of the new moon for best results in feeling refreshed and rested. The benefits to one's state of mind and even one's health are obvious, and doing this on a regular basis, just like exercising regularly, can improve your life and make you feel better mentally, physically, and emotionally—not to mention the side benefit of recharging your magical batteries.

The Short Break

You will need: a bottle of lavender or marjoram essential oil and a reusable water bottle

Bring the bottle of lavender or marjoram essential oil and the water bottle with you wherever you go during the first three days of the dark/new moon, or until you see the first sliver of a crescent. If you cannot use aromatherapy because of allergies or other aversions, just bring the water bottle and make sure it has spring water or filtered tap water in it. Now, every four hours between awakening and going to bed, take a whiff of the oil and/or a drink of water, close your eyes, and imagine your whole body relaxing as the moon slips out of sight into its dark phase. Yes, even if you're a long-distance trucker, I want you to PULL OVER and take a five-minute break! Each day until the crescent moon, repeat this pattern, each time imagining your energy levels coming back gradually just like the moon is coming back as a crescent gradually. It's kind of like a shampoo for the soul: refresh, repeat. Refresh, repeat.

The Long Break

You will need: a private place to relax with little or no electronic interference; a white tea candle and a holder for it; a room where you can see the moon from the window

You will do this in addition to your short break, once a month if possible. Because our Western calendar is not based on the lunar calendar, you will have to check the moon phase. Find a time during the night of the dark moon/new moon phase when you will have two hours' time in which you won't be interrupted. Schedule one of the following for at least some of this time: go to a spa, even if it's just your own bathtub; meditate or follow a guided meditation, visualization, or hypnotherapy session recording; perform progressive relaxation and then fall sleep; or some other *restful* activity that you have found successful in the past.

For these two hours, shut out the rest of the world as much as possible. Don't listen to that "noise" in your head that the Zen practitioners call the "monkey mind"—that obsessive intrusion of words, images, and other thought processes that follows us even when we close our eyes and stop talking. You don't have to spend the whole two hours doing any one thing, just so long as one restful activity is done and the rest of the time you can do as you please … with one qualification: no electronics except what is necessary for the relaxation process, such as a CD player to play a relaxation recording or a clock or watch if you need to set an alarm. No Internet. No cellphone. No texting. No TV. Turn it all off!

Then on the same night either before or after your break as you prefer, light a white tea candle in a holder and go to the room where you can normally see the moon through a window. Look at the moon that isn't there. That's right: unless it's a tiny sliver, look for a moon that's either completely invisible or is just barely visible as a black disk that is slightly darker than the night sky—it's dark moon time! If you don't see any moon at all, you're doing it right!

Now, affirm to yourself that this break, like the break the moon is taking from shining all night, is your monthly time for release and renewal. Hold the candle and speak into the candle everything you want to de-stress from or already have de-stressed from during your two hours. Affirm that you will do this each month, but don't be obsessive about it. Be flexible as to when you take your long break, but even if you have to change the time or date of it, affirm that you will relax each month during some portion of the dark/new moon phase. Then do it!

Rev. **Denise Dumars***, M.A., also known as Dion-Isis, is a Priestess of Isis, Thoth, and Yemaya in the Fellowship of Isis and is a founder of the FOI-chartered Iseum of Isis Paedusis. She is a writer and college professor. She lives in the beautiful beach area near Los Angeles International Airport, but her heart is in New Orleans.*

Illustrator: Rik Olson

Solitary Sabbats for Nonsolitary Pagans

Barbara Ardinger, Ph.D.

Sometimes it happens that our Muggle life gets in the way of our Pagan life. We can't help it. We live in a busy world where there's always too much to do, even on sabbats. How often can we get together on the actual day of the sabbat? Isn't it usually on the closest weekend? Is it hard to find time even on weekends? I've been a member of a ritual group for about ten years. We're spread out in three counties in Southern California, so wherever we meet, it's an hour's drive for some of us. That's one reason some of us are occasionally loath to give up most of one "productive" day for a ritual.

But then other misfortunes befall us, too. A few days before Samhain last year, Jon, one of the group's founders, injured his back. He managed to remain more or less upright for the ritual, but by the time we were feasting, he was crawling into bed. He was still in pain and unable to sit up at Yule, and some of us had other things going on in our lives, so a quick phone consensus was reached to not meet for a ritual. At Imbolc, Jon had just had surgery. No ritual. When the spring equinox arrived, he and his wife had just learned that his elderly parents were very ill. They had to travel to another state to make some life decisions about the parents. Someone else was traveling for business. No ritual. Beltane was the parents' moving day into assisted living. No ritual. Now we're looking at the Summer Solstice and hoping we can get it together. We're friends. We're not solitaries. We crave our ritual time together. (But as I write this, it doesn't look hopeful.)

Your life is busy, too, so what can you do if you're not a solitary? How do you properly celebrate a sabbat if you're unaccustomed to doing solitary rituals or even being alone on a holy day? What can we do when we're forced into temporary solitude? As I see it, we have two choices: do nothing or do something.

Doing nothing has several permutations. You can pretty much ignore the sabbat and go on about your business. It's likely, however, that before the end of the day, you will suddenly stop whatever

How do you properly celebrate a sabbat if you're unaccustomed to doing solitary rituals or even being alone on a holy day? What can we do when we're forced into temporary solitude?

you're doing and remember your ritual circle. Hey, it's Beltane. Happy Beltane, world! That's the bare minimum, and it's good to remember that Pagans do not worship a jealous, angry god. No god will hurl thunderbolts at us if we don't hold a full ritual. The Goddess will still love us when we're not doing anything.

You can do nothing, but do it mindfully. Do whatever you need to do on that day, but pay attention to what you're doing. As you're washing dishes or the car, catching up on your email or doing your expense report, practice the presence of the Goddess. Give your task the careful attention it deserves. Dedicate it to Her and attend to every detail in the very best way you know how. In what tiny way does what you're doing relate to the meaning of the sabbat? What can you do to make this task more magical? Can you feel any divine guidance? At the very least, give your work the same care and attention you'd be giving your part of the ritual.

Here's another way to do nothing mindfully. When the time of day arrives when your group customarily gathers, turn off the TV and all your electronic toys and find a quiet place. This can be your living room or outdoors in a garden or park. Sit quietly. You don't need to fall into a deep, oblivious meditation. Just sit quietly. If you like, visualize the faces of your circle mates and in your imagination see them gathering in the usual place. What magical working would your group be doing today? Do that magical work in your mind. Be methodical and don't skip anything. Enact the whole ritual in your imagination. If you're not gathered in "real life" because someone is ill or traveling, also send healing or other helpful energy. Do "nothing" this way for as long as the nothing requires.

You'll probably agree, however, that it's better to do *something* on a sabbat. When you're alone and not accustomed to being alone, there are lots of somethings you can do. Here are some suggestions.

If you really, really want a ritual, the obvious thing to do is to either go to a public ritual or wrangle an invitation from a friend who belongs to another circle or coven. If you don't get out a lot, public rituals and outer court rituals performed by other traditions will show you that other people do perfectly interesting things. You'll get ideas you can take back to your own group. You can find public rituals listed online and advertised in metaphysical stores. You can also ask around. While you're there, of course, be present and polite and friendly.

If you know ahead of time that your group wouldn't be meeting, go to the library or a bookstore or visit a friend who has so many books her house is sinking into the ground. Select a spiritual book to read on the day of the sabbat. But don't just reach for the newest "wheel of the year" or "how to hold a sabbat" or "try these nifty spells" publication. Go for an old book. Spend at least part of the day reading, say, one of the New Thought or scholarly books written in the last century. Suggestions: *Aradia, or the Gospel of the Witches* (1899) by Charles Godfrey Leland. *Man: Whence, How and Whither: A Record of Clairvoyant Investigation* (1913) by Annie Besant and C. W. Leadbeater (which may be the strangest book I've ever read). Charles Francis Stocking's New Thought novels like *Thou Israel*, which was published in 1921. *The Secrets of Dr. Taverner* (1926) by Dion Fortune. Or any of her other books, either fiction (start with *The Sea Priestess*, 1938) or nonfiction (*The Mystical Qabalah*, 1935). *The Secret Teachings of All Ages* (originally published in 1928) by Manly P. Hall. *The Betty Book* (1937) and *The Unobstructed Universe* (1940) by Stewart Edward White (beautiful books). *The Great Mother* (1947) by Erich Neumann. A *Christian Rosenkreutz Anthology* (1968) edited by Paul M. Allen and containing material that goes back to the seventeenth century. *The Magical Revival* (1973) by Kenneth Grant. I've just pulled all these books off my own shelves. I also found them on Amazon.

Why seek out old books? You've read the third edition of *The Spiral Dance* and all the newer tomes, including those on Pagan and Wiccan history, but what do you know of our high literary roots? What came before our modern Neopaganism? The old books will bend your mind in whole new directions. They'll open new windows in your head, and when you look out, you'll see a whole 'nother universe. Spend your lonely sabbat reading one of these old books, and you won't feel lonely at all. Besides, you'll have something nifty to talk about the next time your group meets.

Another something to do is good works. So-called acts of God are happening all around the world and in every season with no regard for holy days or holidays. People are suffering the after-effects of earthquakes, tsunamis, floods, tornados, hurricanes, fire, famine, and crazy people with weapons. At a minimum, go to www.redcross .org and make a generous donation. Make another donation to an animal rescue agency or to send a kid to camp. Or simply clean out your closets and shelves. Find good clothing or dishes or books or DVDs to donate. (Do not donate junk. Would you like to receive someone else's shabby T-shirts?) Take your donations to a Goodwill or Salvation Army store or a rescue mission or other agency. What else? Participate in a rally or march or campaign for a cause you support. Visit a retirement residence or a hospital and find out what you can do to cheer someone up. If you do this, then neither of you will be alone on this sabbat. But don't preach about the Pagan way. Be present and be friendly.

Finally, in case you've never done a solitary ritual, this is a good time to give it a try. You already know the basics—consider the theme of the sabbat and who to invoke, and decide what your magical working should be. Set up your altar. Do the whole ritual yourself, all the parts. Speak the invocations out loud. Walk around the

circle. Hold the tools. You'll find that it's different from working with your group.

At the end, after you've opened the circle, stay in the room and sit quietly as the energy dissipates. When you've entered your alpha state, run through the ritual you just enacted again, but this time only in your head. What (beyond the obvious) made your solitary ritual different from your customary group rituals? How, for example, is the energy different? As you sit quietly, invoke the Goddess again and ask Her how your solitary ritual looked to Her. Listen carefully to Her reply. Spend as much time in your meditation as you need until you come closer to understanding how members of ritual groups can do perfectly good rituals by themselves.

Barbara Ardinger, Ph.D. (*www.barbaraardinger.com*), *is the author of* Secret Lives, *a novel about a circle of crones, mothers, and maidens, plus goddesses, a talking cat, and the Green Man. Her earlier books include* Pagan Every Day, Goddess Meditations, Finding New Goddesses (*a parody of goddess encyclopedias*), *and* Quicksilver Moon (*a realistic novel … except for the vampire*). *Her day job is freelance editing for people who have good ideas but don't want to embarrass themselves in print. To date, she has edited more than 250 books, both fiction and nonfiction, on a wide range of topics. Barbara lives in Southern California with her two rescued Maine coon cats, Heisenberg and Schroedinger.*

Illustrator: Bri Hermanson

The Electronic BOS

Boudica

We all have them. Notebooks crammed with material we have copied off the web or out of books that we reference again and again in our practice. We have shelves of books, notebooks, and sheets of papers in folders that we really do want to keep; or maybe not. I used that spell, well, maybe two, or was it three, years ago and it worked well, but I forgot what I used it for and I thought I remembered it worked well, but maybe some of those notes in the margins, scribbled quickly …

Some of us may have a mess of notes. I know I did. Well, I still do to be honest. It is going to take a long time to get my BOS sorted out. Recipes, spells, chants, rituals, poems, miscellaneous writings, material copied from the web, pictures—all for my own private use. And I do use them. I am, after all, a practicing Witch.

So how can we organize this better? Well, many of us have a great tool at our disposal yet we never think of using it … our computer or laptop or tablet or smartphone. How about an e-BOS (electronic Book of Shadows)? Oh, you tried that years ago, and now you have CDs with info on them that you can't read. But the technology is much better and storage is simpler to do and just as easy to back up and keep safe.

So let's start with the mess. I am sure, as I have material on both my computer and on paper, that you face the same issue. How to

sort this all out and make sense of it? Let's start with software and work our way up the line.

Word processing programs are available for many folks at no cost, or low cost. Open Source software is free for personal use. Open Office provides several mediums to work with: word processor, presentation program, and graphics program. There is more, but for what we are looking to do here, these are all the basics you will need.

If you are interested in Microsoft Office, that is available at huge discounts to students through Microsoft Student and Microsoft Office Professional Academic. The software is available through their website and offers Office with Word, OneNote, PowerPoint, and more to ALL students, including non-traditional students.

Much of this is available to use on mobile devices as well, available as downloadable apps, and pricing may vary. But the basics needed here is really just a word processing program of some kind.

Much of this is available to use on mobile devices as well, available as downloadable apps, and pricing may vary. But the basics needed here is really just a word processing program of some kind.

A big advantage would be to have a program that creates .pdf files. This kind of program allows you to create .pdf files from any website, complete with the website address (URL). This would allow you to track and, when needed, quote your resource. Some of these features are built into OneNote, where anything you copy is also "stamped" with a URL of the site it came from. A .pdf program allows you to "print" to a .pdf file, which opens with Adobe Reader. There are PDF creators on line for free, and Adobe Reader is also a free program. Or you can purchase Adobe Acrobat to create and edit .pdf files. This will also eliminate lots of paper and ink.

Why track URLs? Why would you care where it came from? Well, for purposes of identifying the material you are saving. Look at the paperwork you have already collected. Do you know where it all came from? Some printouts may have a URL on it, but it may be abbreviated or hard to trace. And if you decide to share, are you sure you wrote that spell or was it copied from somewhere?

This brings us to a brief discussion on copyrights. You are free to use anything "for your own personal use." That means for you and you alone. Not to be copied to a blog, a website, Facebook, or anywhere else. You can copy anything to your computer, use it, print it out, and keep it in your own personal folders. But you can't publish it or share it in a public forum. So keep tabs on what is yours and what belongs to someone else, and you will never end up embarrassed. Enough said.

So let's start sorting through your paperwork.

First, how old is it? Old material can sometimes be good, or sometimes be so much donkey dust. It depends on how far you have advanced and what you have learned thus far. And who wrote it. Make a choice. Keep it, or throw it away because it doesn't apply anymore.

Do you know where it came from? If not, you can either look it up on the web, or you can throw it away. I am sure you will find something better once you start researching again to fill up your new e-BOS.

Does it mean anything to you? It's all well and good that you have it, but really, did you ever use it? Do you still relate to it? Does it mean something special or unique to you and you alone? If so, then it is worth cherishing. If not, throw it away.

And as you go through your paperwork, you are going to find duplicates. Throw away the duplicates. You don't need six copies of "Charge of the Goddess." Or three copies of that Pagan light bulb joke. You will be surprised how often we print something out, simply because over the years we knew we had seen that already but can't find the copy we had. Or you don't realize that it's the same thing again; as it seems new to you, so you print it out or save it again. If  you are unsure you had seen that piece of paper earlier, don't worry about it; we are going to sort through this paperwork and file system one more time to get it into working order.

On your computer, let's address your filing system. Umm, you do have a filing system for all your files, right? A system of naming files and folders so you can find things? I thought so. Let's start fresh and work on a system to file, back up, and find your files.

You can save your files to your hard drive. That is, if it is big enough, if it is new enough, and if you trust your computer. I have external hard drives. These have become so cheap that I have found uses for many different drives. I save to my hard drive and I then back it up onto external drives, which gives me a duplicate system for all my files. Invest in an external hard drive. They are small, they are cheap, and they are easy to hook up: plug and play is wonderful. This will be the critical backup you need to keep your e-BOS and all your other essential files safe and available. Spend money where it counts. Sometimes it's a good idea to spend a few bucks to save time and energy and your precious memories.

Next, how do you set up your filing system? I can make suggestions, but in the end you will find or devise a system that works for you. But, I can give some helpful hints that will assist you in getting started.

How would we want to file away our information? By topic! So let's create some topics. How about starting with MyeBOS as the top file? Start clean with an empty file. And then add into that from elsewhere on your computer and add your paperwork. Inside MyeBOS start your subtopics: spells, recipes, chants, songs, prayers, rituals, photos, pictures. Make these folder names very basic; you can get more specific within these topics.

OK, what about your actual files? Do you name them to match the content, or are they a mishmash of files with names that don't seem to make much sense? We can fix this by creating a system of file naming. All mine have a date, written in year, month, and day. Why? I hate outdated information. I also like to know when I wrote something, or when I first catalogued that piece of information. Then I catalog what the item is. Spell, recipe, chant, song. And a further topic, Hekate or protection, or chicken soup. Yes, I include recipes in my BOS because there is nothing more magical than a meal made to be memorable, happy, healing or comforting; you get the idea.

So my file names can look like this: spell.protection.redbrick dust.20050609.doc. Please be aware that naming conventions on different computers will vary and you will need to adjust your names to fit what your computer will accept. For something someone else wrote: spell.swifting.morrison.2010.docx. You can save rituals in a similar way: yule.for2.20071222.pdf, referencing a Yule for two I wrote for the web in December 2007. How about a picture? I like to add the name of the artist or those pictured and the year the picture was taken: oracle.collier.jpg. Remember, this is a suggestion only. You may find a way that works even better for you.

So what about filing all that paper? Well, we do the same thing—start sorting out the paper into piles like your files. Once you have gone through everything, you have three options. First, find the same article on the web. You may get lucky with Google searches. When you find it, print the webpage to a .pdf file and save it with the appropriate name in the appropriate MyeBOS location. Recycle the paper. Or, you can scan the paperwork into your computer using a scanner—they're very cheap these days and come built into many printers. Again, scan and save as a .pdf, name appropriately, and file away.

The last resort is to re-copy the material by hand. Yes—type it into a word processing program. This will take time, but it can be done. It's good typing practice, and it will allow you to learn how to use the many features of the word processing program you have.

When you find something you want to save, you can use these pictures to embellish your e-documents by adding them to the files.

Now for some ideas on what to do with your new e-BOS! You can save pictures from the web that you feel are pretty, appropriate, or just touch you in the right way. And when you find something you want to save, you can use these pictures to embellish your e-documents by adding them to the files. Adding graphics to documents has become very easy, and you can make your BOS pretty as well as functional. For frequently used files, print them and slide them in a protective plastic sleeve to place in a binder! If it gets dirty or worn, replace from the file on your computer.

A friend of mine purchased a handmade BOS. Beautiful embossed cover, lovely paper inside, well bound. It cost a fortune and she was very delighted with it. But the book did not allow her to insert pages. It was pre-bound, and she didn't want to actually "write" in it, as she felt she would probably mess it up. I suggested she get some specialty papers either from the office supply store or from the hobby shop and then design her work in a processing program, pick a script that was both legible and elegant, type her BOS entry, and add pictures and graphics. Then print the pages out. She could glue them to the book pages or insert them between the pages so she could take them out and use them. She thought that an excellent idea! You can do the same with scrapbooks or other books purchased from stores with blank pages. Your e-BOS does not have to be confined to your computer.

There are so many ideas you can come up with for arranging and using your saved material. And with today's technology, you can save just about anything for your own personal use. Just be sure to keep track of where you got it from, and always give the original author or artist credit. From this you can create a hard copy or electronic keepsake that can be passed on from generation to generation.

Boudica *co-owns* The Wiccan/Pagan Times, *an online Pagan e-zine, with her husband and also runs the* Zodiac Bistro, *an e-zine focused on the Solitary Practitioner. She is a native New Yorker who has been displaced to the wilds of mid-Ohio. Boudica has self-published one spell e-book and is currently working on a series of Reiki teaching e-books (she is a Reiki Master/Teacher) and a fictional piece. She donates time to other sites that promote reading and self-publishing and assists other writers in achieving their own goal of writing and self-publishing. She is a working Witch of over thirty years and now prefers the solitary experience and her own personal spirituality. She lives with her husband of many years and eight cats.*

Illustrator: Christa Marquez

The Witching Hour

Blake Octavian Blair

Midnight and the dark hours surrounding it are a mysterious and celebrated time amongst magickal people. This time period of the day is often dubbed the witching hour. The magickal moment of 12 a.m. marks the changing of one day to another, a gateway, a portal, a cusp. Darkness blankets the land and the sounds of nature play like a symphony, each in part, the trees rustling form their own natural woodwind chorus, the crickets chirping out their own string section riffs, and even the occasional hooting owl is like an elusive saxophone solo in the night.

The moon high in the sky hovers above, observant of it all like a silvery cosmic conductor. Despite all of this, midnight can seem to be quite silent. However, be still with yourself and let your senses sharpen. The magick of the witching hour is palpable—energy and life are buzzing, for Mother Earth never sleeps.

Granted, a good many of us usually are asleep at this time. There are those who must work the night shift and also those who are self-professed night owls, but the vast majority of the human population is slumbering soundly. This is in no small part why the midnight hours provide a good time to do workings under the cover of darkness. It is much easier to deposit spell materials at crossroads and cemeteries when they are clear from bustling traffic and possible onlookers! Historically during eras and in areas where it was dangerous to your life to be known as a Witch, if you were clad in a dark robe you needed only to slip into the safety of the shadowy darkness to become invisible to the threat of possible discovery. Another practical provision this time of day provides is an opportunity to set up for meditative path-working in peaceful quiet, when other members of your household are asleep.

Historically the term "witching hour" is said to have European origins. Some traditions specifically allot the hour of midnight on the night of the full moon as the witching hour; others say it is the hour prior the 12 a.m.; others designate a large window of time at various points in the middle of the night, regardless of moon phase. Clearly there is some leeway as to when you can utilize the energy of the witching hour. Perhaps we could more accurately adapt the term to the plural, witching hours. What is agreed upon is that the connection to the moon is undeniable and the term has long-standing ties to ancient cultures worshipping moon goddesses of fertility and witchcraft. Critics of witchcraft often cast an undesirable light upon the term and the activities associated with it, saying that 3 a.m.

(a time popularly cited within various traditions' time windows for the witching hour) is associated with the devil and evil forces, while 3 p.m. in contrast is associated with benific forces and the crucifixion of the Christ. As Witches we feel this is a grave malignment of the term. In fact 12 a.m. is often considered a point of balance marking the beginning of the day, in contrast to 12 p.m., which marks the middle of the day. It is the contrast of the radiant masculine energy of the midday sun and the powerful feminine energy of the midnight moon. This provides another benefit for working magic at midnight: its energy is wonderful for use in workings that aim to achieve any goals you may have relating to balance. Many of us traditionally work such spells on the equinoxes. However, Mother Nature only allots us two equinoxes per year; the energy of midnight can be used as a suitable substitute at other times of need.

You may well be a diurnal person and sitting here reading this wondering, "All this is well and good, but I need to have my head firmly planted on my pillow at these hours!" Hey, don't worry, I know where you are coming from; I'm a diurnal person as well. But hear me out while I present a few reassuring points of redemption. First, very few workings must be done at these hours. Second, most of us could accommodate a late night here or there once in a while. You certainly won't find me in robes calling the Watchtowers at 12:30 a.m. on any random night of the week. It is a rare occurrence for me to deliberately wait until these times, but they do occur, and those types of situations are what we are speaking of. (Let's see a show of hands: who stays up for a New Year's Eve countdown?) Third, not all spell workings you will need to perform at this time will take you terribly long. Oftentimes, if you can make it to midnight and perform your fifteen minutes (or less) of magick, you're good to go, and quite possibly still in bed in time to get six or so hours of sleep. That may or may not be your personal average, but for an occasional night most will function fine with that amount of slumber. Always remember that your magic need not be complicated to be effective!

I suppose now would be a good time to discuss what types of situations or magickal workings would call for being done during the witching hours. One of the first instances that may come to mind are new moon and full moon rituals. It is not by any means required to wait until darkness to perform all of your new and full moon rites. However, for certain workings, you might find it desirable to actually wait until the moon is high in the night sky, shining down upon your ritual to allow you to more easily mesh with its divine energies. It is a rather glorious experience to be working magic while looking up and working under the moon in all her shining glory. You may also wish to consecrate items under the moonlight, in which case you may stay up and wait until the witching hours to perform the initial blessing and consecration ceremony. Sure, you could simply lay the item in the windowsill and it will indeed effectively be blessed and cleansed by the moonlight, but the moonlit ceremony would certainly add an extra energetic oomph to the act! Fertility rituals were historically and are often still performed during night hours with the reasoning that the light of the full moon is associated with fertility. It is thought that letting the moon's light pour upon your body or perhaps your fields during the ritual will impart the blessings of fertility on not only the physical but all levels. As mentioned earlier, many start the witching hours at 11 p.m.

so as to include the hour leading up to midnight, allowing you to perhaps perform your rite on the way to bed.

The nighttime hours also have a long association with communication with the spirit world. The moon is associated with psychic abilities, and its presence during these hours provides a welcome enhancement to this type of work. Séances are commonly planned around the witching hour, as this is also considered the time when the veil between the worlds is thin. All these factors combined make these late-night and early morning hours perfectly suited to contacting the other side. It is no coincidence that Samhain rituals are most popularly performed at night. (Note: Séances and other spirit work should be undertaken carefully and with protections in place.)

You may wish to try your hand at moon scrying. The supply list is short and uncomplicated. Simply gather a fair-sized bowl (a salad, fruit, or punch bowl works well) and fill it with water (I prefer purified or spring water) on a moonlit night. Water is a wonderful lunar divination tool, since the connection between the moon and the tides is well known. Many prefer a full moon for this divination, although it is not required. Simply set up in an outdoor area in which you will not be disturbed and where you are positioned under the light of the moon. Feel free to smudge and create a sacred space as you see fit. Bring yourself into a place of inner calm and gaze into the reflective surface of the water. Let the images and impressions come to you and trust your intuition. When you are finished, pour the water onto the base of a tree to nourish the land. You may wish to record your experiences into your Book of Shadows or other journal.

Those practitioners who engage in energetic healing work of any kind will find that working at night provides a different energetic working environment than do daytime sessions. Contrary to

many mainstream associations, darkness is not necessarily scary; sometimes being cloaked in the dark of night can be an exceptionally healing and transformative space to be in. If you work with the chakras, the moon is associated with the second or sacral chakra. It is then not surprising that moonstone works well as a healing crystal at the second chakra. If needed you can utilize your nighttime healing sessions in conjunction with the phases of the moon to work on the sacral chakra and for using one's desires and ambitions for manifesting physical change and action.

The concept of the witching hour can be traced back to ancient worship of goddesses with lunar ties such as Artemis, Selene, Cerridwen, and Hekate. The hours of the night are especially sacred to the Dark Mothers.

As mentioned earlier, the concept of the witching hour can be traced back to ancient worship of goddesses with lunar ties such as Artemis, Selene, Cerridwen, and Hekate. The hours of the night are especially sacred to the Dark Mothers. Hekate is perhaps one of the most popular deities among practitioners of the Craft and has long been heralded as the Queen of the Witches with associations with the moon as well as the spirit world. She bears torches of illumination while navigating the darkness. Many of her devotees thus prefer to perform their devotions and workings with her during the dark hours. Her rites are also commonly made more practically executable at night. Hekate holds three-way crossroads sacred and presides over them. Crossroads are often the preferred location for performing rituals to her and/or for leaving offerings to her. These types of activities are clearly made easier not only when you have the cover of darkness but also when foot, auto-traffic, and other onlookers and disturbances are typically at a minimum.

It is also helpful to know that you are by no means limited to working with female deities for your nighttime rituals, as there are male deities with lunar associations. The cosmology of the Norse ascribes the nighttime hours to the masculine Divine. The Norse god Mani is thought of as the moon personified. The Hindu god Shiva is a lunar deity. He even wears the crescent moon as an adornment among his dreadlocks, which is said to symbolize his mastery of the mind. Shiva is the god of the timeless cycle of creation and destruction as well as the perception of reality. This cycle is often seen as analogous to the waxing and waning cycles of the moon. He is eternal and a god of the dead, known for meditating in the cremation grounds. These factors combined make him an excellent choice of a more masculine energy to work with for lunar and nighttime workings.

Of course nobody said that all of your nocturnal workings and rituals had to be done in a waking state. The dream realm can be one of the most powerful arenas for astral travel, spirit visitation, insight, and path-working. In Haitian Vodou dreaming is one of the primary forms of divination. A wonderful magickal act is to keep a dream journal of these experiences. This also serves as a way to honor the sacred work you perform during your dream state. After you've chosen the book you will use as your journal, perform a consecration ceremony for it, preferably under a new or full moon. Then keep your dream journal beside your bed with a pen so that you can easily and promptly record your experiences if you should wake in the middle of the night or when the alarm goes off in the morning.

To aid you in your dream-time work and journeys you may wish to call upon one of the many deities that have dominion over the dream world. For example, the Greek goddess Asteria holds sway over the magic of the night. She not only holds dreaming as one of her specialties but specifically may be petitioned when prophetic dreams are desired. Archangel Michael is often summoned to protect one from or to banish nightmares. Consider setting up your own bedside shrine to your dream-time deity of choice. Say a bedtime prayer to the deity and leave them offerings there. You can even use it as an appropriate place to store your dream journal.

. . . .

We can all access the power of the witching hours. There are as many approaches to working with its energy as there are ways to practicing the Craft itself. One need not be nocturnal (or even awake, for that matter!) to effectively utilize the powerful energy of the night. With a dash of planning, a healthy dose of creativity, and a good measure of classic Pagan resourcefulness, you will be well on your way to powerful experiences of your own in the witching hours!

RESOURCES

D'Este, Sorita. *Hekate: Keys to the Crossroads.* London: Avalonia, 2006.

Grimassi, Raven. *Encyclopedia of Wicca & Witchcraft: 2nd Edition Revised and Expanded.* St. Paul, MN: Llewellyn, 2003.

Guiley, Rosemary Ellen. *The Encyclopedia of Witches & Witchcraft: Second Edition.* New York: Checkmark Books, 1999.

Illes, Judika. *Encyclopedia of Spirits: The Ultimate Guide to the Magic of Fairies, Genies, Demons, Ghosts, Gods & Goddesses.* New York: Harper One, 2009.

Judith, Anodea. *Wheels of Life: Revised and Expanded Edition.* St. Paul, MN: Llewellyn, 1999.

Krasskova, Galina. *Exploring the Northern Tradition: A Guide to the Gods, Lore, Rites, and Celebrations from the Norse, German, and Anglo-Saxon Traditions.* Franklin Lakes, NJ: New Page Books, 2005.

Blake Octavian Blair's *full bio appears on page 91.*

Illustrator: Tim Foley

Simple Kitchen Alchemy

Deborah Blake

When most of us think of witchcraft, we probably envision a ritual under the light of the full moon or a coven gathering for a sabbat celebration like Samhain or Beltane. And those are certainly important elements of a magickal practice … but they are only the tip of the iceberg.

The Witches of old didn't just practice the Craft on holidays and full moons; it was a part of their everyday lives, integrated into much of what they did on a daily basis. Protection might have been woven into the fabric of a child's clothing as it was spun on a wheel and stretched on a loom, and particular crops were planted under a waxing or waning moon to ensure a good harvest.

Cooking is the perfect way to add a little magick to your everyday life, with no one the wiser. It is something you likely do anyway, so it won't take much of an effort to put this extra magickal boost into your schedule. And we often use herbs and spices in our daily cooking, most of which have specific magickal properties that can be utilized to create what I like to call kitchen alchemy.

Alchemy is the art of mixing various ingredients that then magickally transform into something greater—and doesn't the cook aim to do just that? Whether you are preparing a snack for yourself or a fancy spread for guests or a healthy meal for your family, you can add an extra touch that will transform your food into something truly magickal for heart, health, and home.

Some Basic Ingredients

Almost everything in your refrigerator and kitchen cabinets has some magickal association. Here are a few of the most common and easiest to integrate into everyday meals. These associations are based primarily on *Cunningham's Encyclopedia of Wicca in the Kitchen*—if you only get one resource, I highly recommend this one. But different sources give various other associations; always follow your own internal wisdom when it comes to witchcraft.

Apple: love, health, peace
Basil: love, protection, prosperity
Beans: prosperity, sexuality
Black pepper: protection, purification
Cayenne pepper: energy, creativity
Chocolate: love, prosperity
Cinnamon: love, psychic awareness, prosperity
Coffee: conscious mind, physical energy
Dill: conscious mind, prosperity, weight loss, love
Garlic: protection, health
Ginger: love, prosperity
Lemon: love, happiness, purification
Milk: love, spirituality
Olives (and olive oil): health, peace, sexuality, spirituality
Parsley: prosperity, protection, sexuality
Peppermint: healing, purification, sexuality
Pomegranate: creativity, fertility, prosperity
Potato: protection
Rosemary: conscious mind, healing, love, protection
Sage: health, protection
Salt: grounding, protection
Spinach: prosperity
Sugar/honey/maple syrup: love, prosperity
Thyme: love, psychic ability, purification
Tomato: health, love, prosperity, protection
Vanilla: love, sexuality

How Kitchen Alchemy Works

Kitchen alchemy is really a very simple form of magickal work; it doesn't require circle casting or the invocation of elements, and you don't even need to use a spell for most basic everyday dishes. (You may want to use one for the truly important occasions, like having your boss to dinner or the first meal you cook for a new lover, but that's up to you.)

Like all magick, kitchen alchemy is primarily a matter of intent, focus, and will. You start by choosing your intention—increasing prosperity, for instance, or creating an atmosphere of love and peace in your home. Then, as you are cooking, you add the magickal ingredients you have chosen to use while focusing on your intention and directing your will into the dish. As with other magickal workings, the more intent, focus, and will you bring to your food preparation, the more effective your kitchen alchemy will be.

Now that you know how simple it is, let's get cooking!

Magickal Mocha

Here is one of my favorite examples of kitchen alchemy; I make this one for myself almost every day, and it is the perfect jump-start to my morning. You will want to adjust the spices and sugar to suit your tastes.

Ingredients

- 1 cup coffee (prepared) OR 1 teaspoon instant coffee, for energy and focus

- 1 cup milk (or more, if using instant coffee), for love and faith

- 2–3 tablespoons hot chocolate mix (use good hot chocolate made with real chocolate, or substitute cocoa and add more sugar), for love and prosperity

- 1 teaspoon sugar (or more), for sweetness in life

- Pinch of cinnamon, for love and prosperity

- Pinch of cayenne pepper, for energy and creativity

- *Optional*: a drop or two of vanilla, for sensuality and love

Magickal goals: love, prosperity, energy, creativity (these are all things I work toward every day, although some days I focus more on one than another)

To *prepare*

I use a coffee maker to make the coffee, although some days I just prepare instant coffee instead. All the other ingredients are put in a hot chocolate machine, and then I add the flavored hot chocolate to the coffee. You can easily do this in a pot on the top of the stove. I start with the milk, then add all the other ingredients one by one, saying aloud the properties I want as I go (for example, "energy and creativity" as I sprinkle in the cayenne pepper). If you are making this in a pot, make sure you are stirring clockwise. Pour into a mug and raise your cup to the goddess in thanks before drinking.

$PINACH $ALAD

If you need a financial boost, try this salad full of ingredients that work for prosperity. It's good for you, too!

Ingredients

- 1 cup raw spinach per person (spinach is often sprayed with chemicals, so get organic if you can); use baby spinach or tear larger leaves into small pieces

- ⅓ cup chopped tomato per person

- ¼ cup candied almonds or pecans, for prosperity

- Fresh basil to taste (don't use dried basil—it will work for the magick but won't taste right)

- Fresh parsley to taste

- Optional: fresh dill to taste

- Shredded parmesan cheese

- Sunflower seeds (about a teaspoon)

- Olive oil and balsamic vinegar OR the salad dressing of your choice

Magickal goal: prosperity

To prepare
Wash all greens and drain or dry well. Place the spinach in a bowl and add all other ingredients one at a time, focusing on prosperity as you add each one. If you have a particular need (for example, if you are job hunting, or have a large bill to pay), you may want to visualize that need being fulfilled as you prepare the salad. Top with dressing and enjoy.

BAKED APPLE BLISS

Here is a simple and healthy dessert you can make for yourself or for those you love. Remember that love magick isn't just about romantic love, although it certainly can work for that too! Just focus on your particular intention, whether it is to draw love in or give it to someone else.

Ingredients
- 1 apple per person, cored but otherwise intact

- 1 tablespoon of maple syrup OR honey (sugar will work in a pinch)

- Cinnamon to taste

- *Optional*: $1/8$ teaspoon vanilla extract (make sure it's real vanilla extract and not vanilla flavoring), for romantic love magick

- *Optional*: chopped brazil nuts or pistachios

Magickal goal: to open yourself or someone else to love (without interfering with free will!), to give love to another or to yourself

To prepare

Core the apple using an apple corer or a knife. Place the apple in a heat-safe dish. If using the nuts, place them inside the cavity of the apple. Pour the syrup or honey inside the apple and over the top (mix the vanilla into the syrup or honey first, if using); sprinkle with cinnamon. Hold your hands over the apple and close your eyes. Concentrate on feeling love in your heart and sending it into the apple. If working to draw love in, feel your heart opening up to the love of the Goddess and whatever else the universe has to offer. Then bake the apple (or apples) in the oven at 375 degrees F for 30 or 40 minutes, depending on the size of the apple. You can also microwave the apple(s) on high for 4 to 8 minutes. The length of time will depend on the size of the apple, how many you are baking, and the power of your microwave, so start with 4 minutes and then do another minute or two at a time, checking for doneness periodically. Apples should be tender (a fork goes in easily) but not mushy.

CLEAR MY KARMA LEMONADE

Lemons are wonderful for purification and happiness, which makes them the perfect food for anyone who is trying to diet or get healthy. For a cooling summer drink with an extra magickal boost, try making a pitcher of this sparkling lemonade.

Ingredients

- 2 lemons, juiced

- ¼–½ cup of sugar (more or less depending on your desired sweetness—if using the prosecco or champagne instead of seltzer, use less sugar); if you want to make the sugar mix with the lemon more easily, you can dissolve it into a little water on the stove and make a simple syrup

- 3–4 cups of seltzer OR a sparkling wine like prosecco or champagne

- *Optional*: a few sprigs of fresh mint or a drop or two of rosewater (watch out—it is very powerful stuff!) or a few rose petals

Magickal goal: purification, happiness

To prepare

Squeeze the juice from the lemons and discard any seeds. Add sugar to the lemon juice (it is better to start out with less and add more later if it isn't sweet enough, but you can always add more lemon if you overdo the sugar). As you do so, think about how life is a mixture of the sweet and the tart, and how happiness comes from focusing on the positive. See how bright and vivid the lemon is, and envision the purifying energy of the sun captured in its essence. Pour your lemon/sugar mixture into a pitcher and fill the pitcher the rest of the way with seltzer or prosecco (or a combination, if you want less alcohol). See the bubbles rise up like the joy you feel rising in your spirit on a beautiful summer day. Sprinkle with mint or rose and drink with friends. (Note: to make for one person, reduce amounts and make in a glass instead of a pitcher.) For extra purification magick, visualize the bubbles moving through your body, clearing and cleansing.

Bringing Magick into Your Kitchen Every Day

These recipes are good examples of how you can use kitchen alchemy to create magickal drinks and meals for special occasions. But you don't need to use a particular recipe or wait for a celebration (or a crisis) to work your magick in the kitchen. Like the magickal mocha I make for breakfast each morning, simple kitchen alchemy can be added to your daily routine to bring a little extra magick to the food you eat every day.

With a little research into the magickal qualities of the foods you enjoy and the focus, intent, and will you already use for your other magickal workings, you can practice your Craft in the kitchen and bring new power to your cooking with kitchen alchemy.

Deborah Blake *is the author of* Circle, Coven and Grove: A Year of Magickal Practice, Everyday Witch A to Z: An Amusing, Inspiring & Informative Guide to the Wonderful World of Witchcraft, The Goddess is in the Details: Wisdom for the Everyday Witch, Everyday Witch A to Z Spellbook, *and the* COVR Award–winning Witchcraft on a Shoestring, *all from Llewellyn. She has published numerous articles in Pagan publications, including Llewellyn annuals, and has an ongoing column in* Witches & Pagans Magazine. *Her award-winning short story* "Dead and (Mostly) Gone" *is included in the* Pagan Anthology of Short Fiction: 13 Prize Winning Tales. *Deborah has been interviewed on television, radio, and podcast, and can be found online at Facebook, Twitter, and http://deborahblake.blogspot.com. When not writing, Deborah runs the Artisans' Guild, a cooperative shop she founded with a friend in 1999, and also works as a jewelry maker. She lives in a hundred-year-old farmhouse in rural upstate New York with five cats who supervise all her activities, both magickal and mundane.*

Illustrator: Kathleen Edwards

Moving into New Adventures

Jenett Silver

Moving can be a daunting task at the best of times, but it is particularly challenging for those of us whose spiritual and magical lives are tied to a particular geography, community, or climate. At the same time, a move (whether across town or across the country) can be a wonderful time of renewal, inspiration, and new opportunity. Like so many things in life, it's about what you bring to the experience.

My story of moving—like so many people's—is driven by a new job. In the summer of 2011, I'd been living in

the Twin Cities of Minnesota (Minneapolis and St. Paul) for twelve years. While there, I'd joined a Pagan group and become a priestess and teacher in that tradition. I'd gotten active in Twin Cities Pagan Pride, helped create a new spring conference event (Paganicon), and generally done a lot of other wonderful things and made some great friends. But I'm also a librarian who is as passionate about my profession as I am my religious life, and the realities of the field meant the next stage of my career would probably mean a move. A great university in rural Maine offered me a dream job with duties I love, and it would bring me back within driving distance of family and friends besides.

A month after getting that offer, I was on the road with a good friend, ready to drive halfway across the country with my cat and folk harp in a rented car, and everything I owned in boxes and containers, bracing for lots of changes. I was moving from a major metro area to a rural town. (I live in the largest town in the county, but it's still under eight thousand people.) I was switching the kind of library and students I was working with. And I was moving from a place where there are multiple Pagan events every night of the week to somewhere where driving an hour or three to even meet other Pagans is pretty common.

All of that led me to think about some complicated questions. How does where I live affect my spiritual life? What does it mean to leave the community of my (small) tradition and move somewhere else? And, of course, what witchy and Pagan things could I do to make my move work out for the best in every way possible?

Opening to Possibility

I started thinking about a possible move very early, as an organic part of my job hunt. I focused on the goal of having the right job, with the right people, in a place I could thrive, and where the practical details (things like salary and benefits) would work for me. Each time I looked at an advertisement, I thought about what it would be like to live and work in that place. And I balanced being open minded about location with self-awareness (I wilt in heat, so did not look extensively in the Southern United States, for example).

Each time I had a phone interview, I checked out what it would be like to live in that place in more detail. What would my housing options look like? Which of my hobbies would be easy to do, and which would be harder? And of course, I checked out the local Pagan community, by looking at Witchvox (http://witchvox .com), checking out area Pagan Pride events for links to local groups (http://paganpride.org), and doing some general web searches using terms like "Pagan" or "Witch" and town or region names.

I also listened to my intuition. Each application brought me a new idea about where I might be happy living and working, and what I'd enjoy about being there. I piled these ideas up inside my head like river-tumbled stones: each one delightful but unique, a range of potential outcomes. As I did magical and ritual work, I used that image to help me remember that I was looking for something that had many possible answers. I wanted somewhere I could thrive without my preconceptions getting in the way.

Make Peace with Leaving

Moving is a great time to look at what's working in our lives and what isn't. In some ways, the physical things are the easiest part to deal with. I made a commitment that I'd only move what I loved: everything else went into the donation or recycling piles.

But moving can also send waves of change through relationships. Some friends will be wonderfully supportive (even though they'll miss you). Others may take your decision to move very personally.

You may find that your process goes more smoothly if you don't share every detail with them. Instead, share your joy with the people who can nourish your happiness at finding a new place to grow. And above all, be gentle with any strong emotions that come to the surface, for you or for others. Don't let a few challenging weeks wreck a long friendship.

Take some time to tidy up loose ends. Check in with people you haven't seen for a while from old jobs or projects, and pass on your good news. Send an email or a notecard thanking someone for something you particularly appreciated. Take time to tidy up any projects you're working on. If you're continuing some job tasks after your move (or helping whoever is taking them over), be extra clear about how that's going to work, so everyone's on the same page.

All of this is a slow, steady cleansing ritual, and packing and planning and moving kicks up just as much old energy and energetic connections as dust. For all these reasons, this is a great time to be more deliberate about repeating your favorite cleansing methods a bit more frequently. My favorite is a bath with a handful or so of sea salt thrown in, or using a sea salt–based soap, but there are plenty of other options using essential oils, aura cleansing techniques, or smudging. It's also a great time to cleanse your home as you finish packing a particular room or area.

Last Days

While you'll have lots to do in the final days before your move, build in some time that's about relationships, not just packing. A simple party with friends and loved ones (with some easy food) can be a good way to bring gentle closure. It can be a great way to clear out your pantry, too, both by making party food and by letting friends take home items you don't want to move.

A friend suggested a lovely moving ritual she's used several times. Before she moves, she makes a batch of a flexible recipe for the friends she's leaving behind. Once she's settled in her new home and has made some new connections, she makes that recipe again, adding one new ingredient. That way, she recognizes the continuity of her experience but also makes space for what is new. She does this with lasagna, adding one new thing each move. I chose to make an herb bread, but pasta salads and some kinds of cookies or baked goods also work well.

Another great idea is to take a little time to visit a few favorite places in your old home. I made sure to have meals at the restaurants I'd miss most. (It's particularly handy to do this once you pack your kitchen gear.) The last day before I left, I went down to the place where I'd first fallen in love with Minnesota, the bridge over the Minnehaha Falls, and spent a little time communing with the river and the water. Doing that deliberately helped me feel more comfortable driving away.

Thoughtful packing can also make a big difference in the quality of your move. Think about what things you'll need immediately in your new home (something to sleep on and in, something to help you make and store food, something for the bath or shower). But chances are, there will also be a number of items you don't need immediately (all of your books, off-season clothes, all of your hobby gear). Good packing will help reinforce what's most important to you, as well as make it easy to get settled once you get to your new home.

Finally, make sure you clean up any energetic and magical ties from your home. Some common things to check include retrieving

Witch bottles or other protections on or around your property, preparing any plants you're bringing with you for the move, and harvesting any herbs you want to dry for use before new ones will be ready in your new home. And, of course, you want to pack up your magical and ritual tools. I was moving over the new moon, so part of my final full moon ritual was packing all of my tools away except the ones I use in my daily practice. This packing helped me feel more like the move was ready to take place.

Some common things to check include retrieving Witch bottles or other protections on or around your property, preparing any plants you're bringing with you for the move, and harvesting any herbs you want to dry for use before new ones will be ready in your new home.

As you pack, you may want to set aside a few ritual items that you want to have on hand immediately after you move in. Some traditions say you should only bring a new broom into a new home (never move the one you used before). Salt, honey, and bread show up in a lot of moving traditions as a way to bless a new home. I packed a small basket with some candles, salt, honey, incense, and a few small altar tokens and made sure it was the first thing into the apartment once we'd arrived.

Liminal Time

Moving is a time between times, and it's definitely a time between places. Make the most of that space, which holds a great deal of potential and possibility. This is especially true for a longer move,

like mine, where we spent two and a half days driving. I prepared a range of playlists to listen to, including a very specific playlist for the last hour I was driving into my new hometown. I also had some great conversations with the friend who was helping me with the drive: it was a luxury not to need to run off to do other things, and just be able to talk.

There's also something very soothing about this part of the moving process. So many things in our lives are very complicated, with many overlapping due dates and expectations. But for the time it takes you to get from one home to another, life is pretty simple. You need to drive a certain distance to get to your next stop, when something pretty simple happens (you have a meal, you sleep, you unpack). And then you go on to the next stop.

I found myself really enjoying that simplicity, and wondering how I could keep that feeling once I was settled. In my new home,

I've been cautious about taking on any ongoing commitments. I've chosen to explore a range of things in my new town, from the farmers' market to the local coffee and sandwich shops to local hiking trails. Giving myself simple things to do, without a lot of expectations, has been a lot of fun, as well as a great way to get to know the area better. And it's kinder to my body and spirit in the midst of a great deal of change.

Settling In

Take advantage of the power of the first moments and days in your new home. Begin your new life here the way you'd like to keep going. Start by bringing in the things that are most important to you first (if you possibly can). In my case, that was my small basket of ritual items, my cat, and my folk harp.

Some early ritual activities are also important to me when I move, even if it's just across town. During my first evening in a new home, I do a simple ritual of cleansing and protecting the new space. I bless salt water and incense, and walk the space counterclockwise, pausing to put a pentagram in salt water on each door and window. I also pour a little salt water down each drain (and each toilet) to help cleanse it. Once I'm more settled, I go back and do a more thorough protective ritual, but this way I have a few days to get comfortable with the feel of the space and the energies of that specific location.

The last part of the moving process is making your new location truly your home, and that means making connections. Check out local places where you can meet people who share your hobbies or interests. Consider volunteering for a cause that you care about. Ask people at your new job about the best places for food and fun.

And on the Pagan side, take those links and resources you found way back when you were job searching, and check out what events you might be interested in going to. Even if it's a longer drive than you're up for regularly, consider going to anything you can while you're settling in. It's a great way to meet people. Online resources (like email lists for your state or region, social networking sites, and more) can also help you find people closer to you.

Our connections, of course, aren't just about people. Take time to get to know the place you're now living. Are the seasons different? Even though Maine and Minnesota are at about the same latitude, I found myself surprised that Maine was quite often chilly in the mornings, even in August. And of course, larger seasonal events—when it rains the most, when the first snow might fall, when different plants bloom, what spring or fall feels like—will change from place to place. Nature walks or wildlife guides can be a great way to begin to get more familiar with this part of your new home as well. (And these days, there are some great smartphone apps that can help you identify plants, animal prints, and much more while you're out and about, as well as the more traditional books.)

All moves are unique, just like each ritual brings us new insights. With a little attention, however, our move can become a way to deepen and broaden our spiritual lives, rather than something simply to be endured. Whatever life brings you, see how you can use that spark of change to create the life you want to live going forward.

Jenett Silver *is delighted to be back in New England, and even more delighted to be within range of both ocean and mountains again. A Witch and priestess in a small initiatory religious witchcraft tradition, she's enjoying getting to know a different part of the Pagan community. She blogs at* http://gleewood.org/threshold.

Illustrator: Rik Olson

Magical Transformations

EVERYTHING OLD IS NEW AGAIN

Persephone's Return: Embracing Inner Darkness

Sybil Fogg

When my oldest daughter was fifteen and I was pregnant with my youngest, we had an argument that escalated to the point of her running away. She was assisted by an adult who allowed her to move in and attempted to keep my child away from the rest of our immediate family. I had experienced preterm labor before, so it was not surprising when the same thing happened that November. Fortunately, with the help of my family and my midwives, I was able to hold off and focus on the child I had to bring into the world, whom we welcomed in early December.

Not too long after his birth, I felt the first pangs of postpartum depression. I was familiar with the feeling, as I had experienced it before after a rather traumatizing illness came over my third daughter soon after her birth. After spending that winter running from one doctor's office to another, I broke down. At the time, I allowed myself to sink into the darkness and work my way out again. It was difficult, but I found an inner strength and learned much about my core self. When I felt those feelings again, I decided to embrace the journey inward because I knew where it would lead. With much thought and meditation, I realized that my inward and then outward spiral was similar to that of an old Greek myth I was familiar with: the story of Persephone's descent.

With much thought and meditation, I realized that my inward and then outward spiral was similar to that of an old Greek myth … the story of Persephone's descent.

The story I remember learning about Persephone did not do much to demonstrate her feminism or sensuality. It began with her out picking flowers with a group of nymphs on one of those kind of spring days where the air caresses skin and the grass gives way under the gentle pressure of footsteps. Persephone and her maidens dance and revel in the early warmth and gather blossoms to weave into garlands or among their curls. Persephone wanders away from the group to discover a bloom she had never spied before. Fascinated and greedy, she reaches down to pluck the living jewel. As the root comes free from the soil, the ground splits and Hades emerges.

He plucks Persephone from the meadow and whisks her away to his home deep in Earth's core, determined to keep her as his bride.

Persephone refuses to eat in protest. Her self-inflicted starvation eventually fails, and she eats anywhere from one to six pomegranate seeds. Eating the food of the dead locks her into the Underworld, but fortunately for her, her mother, Demeter, the harvest goddess, pleads with Zeus, the king of the gods, for her daughter's return. Although Zeus has the power to intervene, Persephone has eaten the food of the Underworld, so she cannot simply be returned to the land of the living. As a compromise, she is allowed to live with her mother for a period of time, but then must return to Hades one month for each pomegranate seed she consumed. While she is above ground, Demeter is happy and the ground is fertile and the crops bear fruit. But when Persephone returns to the Underworld, the ground is barren and nothing will grow, giving us our winter. The story emphasizes the strength of Demeter, giving Persephone little play other than as a catalyst for this nature myth.

A spiral into our souls can often be illuminating as we discover new aspects of our personalities and see our own darkness laid bare.

As have many Witches before me, I've striven to claim Persephone as an embodiment of female strength. Since growing up, I have read many accounts of this tale depicting Persephone as a willing Queen of the Underworld, claiming her as one of the dark goddesses. As much as my girl-self (or Kore, as Persephone is often referred to in her maiden incarnation before her descent) longs to hold on to Persephone's representation of light, youth, and innocence, I have had to accept that she harbors a darker side. Part of Persephone's journey is her need to accept this shadow self, since she will forever be entwined with it.

It is apparent that darkness enfolds many of us during the mid-autumn days, dragging us deeper until the first buds of spring emerge. This time of year is ideal for turning inward and spending time with ourselves. A spiral into our souls can often be illuminating as we discover new aspects of our personalities and see our darkness laid bare.

At different times, we all struggle with who we are at our core versus the image we project publicly. I admit there have been moments when I was shocked to unlock certain parts of myself. As Heraclitus stated a millennium ago, "The only constant is change." Sometimes it is integral to our happiness on this planet to work on smoothing out those parts of ourselves we discover when we go

inward in the dark winter months so that we come forth with something new, stronger, wiser, and overall more rounded.

In other instances, it is equally important to acknowledge the darker movements of our soul and to embrace them, because they can make us stronger. When Persephone accepted her role as Queen of the Underworld, she discovered that she had power to assist others such as Hercules and Orpheus in their quests. In other myths, she ruled by her husband's side, taking part in passing judgment and doling out punishments on the shades who passed before her. These shadow aspects of our personalities lie deep within us and can be explored if we take the time to spiral inward.

Winter comes harshly where I live in the Northeast. This time of year is brutal and long. Winter outings at first are exciting and adventurous, but eventually sour as day after day, week after week, and month after month passes with very little change. Although some of us live with a large group of people, we still feel isolated because we automatically gravitate toward an inner realm in the cold months as the world outside our homes grows barren.

How do we determine when it is appropriate to change an aspect of our personality and when we should embrace it? That truly depends on the one doing the meditation. I have gone into myself and have thought I had discovered a true strength only to later develop shock or embarrassment over my feelings or behavior. I am not suggesting that anyone try to overcome a personality trait that they believe others would find lacking or frustrating; this is an exercise for only oneself.

For example, I have discovered that I have a tendency to avoid confrontation. When my daughter walked out of my home, she arranged for a friend to wait around the corner to whisk her away. When I tracked them down, the other parents denied me access to my child. When I arrived at their house, my daughter refused to leave with me. Not wanting to make a scene, I left alone. At home, I would call each day to talk to my child; sometimes she would talk to me and other times she refused. Never once did I vocalize my anger in the situation. I tried to be open and accepting. But I was dealing with an emotional teenager who wasn't equipped to know what was best for her.

In my fear of having a verbal altercation, I did not order my child home. Inside, I knew this passivity was weak and wrong. When I went through my descent, I knew that I had handled the situation incorrectly. I spent time working within myself to lay bare my fears and accept them, enfold them, and then release them. I knew I would never be free of the discomfort a confrontation would create for me, but I understood that I would have to take on the disquiet I feel and work my way through it. When I returned from my meditation, I was stronger. I called my daughter's grandparents and worked out an arrangement to get her out of that other house. I was able to contact the police, obtain a restraining order and follow through to court. I hadn't known before then that I possessed that strength. A few years later, my daughter admitted she was confused and scared. At the time, she had actually wanted me to take charge and had felt great relief when I finally did.

I know I would not have been able to overcome my fear had I not remembered Persephone's descent. This goddess drew from Kore, her maiden self, to give her strength in the darkness until it was time to spiral to the surface. In her time spent in Hades, she learned she had strength in

her core; it was only a matter of tapping into it. We can learn from this myth and do our own descent into the darkness of the earthly realm of winter, embrace our shadow self, and make our way home again—complete.

Sybil Fogg *has been a practicing Witch for over twenty years. She is also known as Sybil Wilen. She chose to use her mother's maiden name in Pagan circles to honor her grandparents. She's also a wife, mother, writer, teacher, and belly dancer. Her family shares her passion for magic, dance, and writing. She lives in South Portland, Maine, with her husband and children. Please visit her website at www.sybilwilen.com.*

Illustrator: Christa Marquez

The Transformative Nature of Hekate

Marion Sipe

While today Hekate is largely regarded as a goddess of Witches
and magic, her roots are as a deity of
transformation. Her place in Greek
history and religion can be hard to decipher because she has played many
roles and been cast in many lights, and
the only thing that never changes is
that she is never quite the same.

Among the ancient Greeks there
was a distinct split between city-
dwellers and country-dwellers. The
urban Greeks generally considered
anything outside the city's walls to be
chaotic and possibly even dangerous.

Hekate's worship took hold among the urban Greeks as a protective matron, the goddess who watched over travelers. For urban Greeks, any place where a decision was required was a point of transformation and therefore an opportunity for things to go wrong. For them Hekate was the goddess who stood beside doors and gates, because once they left their home, decisions were required; Hekate was there to guide them. Once they left the city, there were possible dangers; Hekate stood there as well. At the crossroads, both inside and outside cities, Hekate watched over travelers as they chose their paths.

The rural Greeks were less suspicious of the world around them. They were more closely connected with the land because they worked it every day, so for them Hekate's aspects changed. Hesiod, a rural Greek farmer of around 700 BCE, attributes many *timai* ("honors" or "functions") to Hekate that are not attributed to her by urban writers such as Homer. This may be because the vision of Hekate held by the rural Greeks was inherently different than that held by the urban Greeks. In Hesiod's *Theogony*, Hekate is "honored above all" by Zeus and holds a share of the earth, the sea, and the heavens. She is said to have the power to grant victory in battle or the games, to increase the fecundity of livestock or the catch of the fishermen. She is called the nurse of the young and is said to sit beside kings as they pass judgments. Hesiod may well speak of these aspects of Hekate because they are the ones that were particularly relevant to his life outside of the Greek city.

Despite this inherent disconnect between the urban protectress and the rural fertility goddess, Hekate's honors have much in common with each other. They are all about transformation. They concern the moments in which one thing becomes another, or has the potential to become another, from the conception of cattle to the decisions of kings.

This is still true of the goddess. Today she is seen as a deity of death and the resulting journey beyond the Veil, a goddess of dusk and dawn and the cycles of the moon. Hekate has long been associated with all of these things, and with many different deities, but she remained distinct. She is not merely a goddess of the dawn, despite being tied to it in Homer's *Hymn to Demeter*. She is not just a goddess of the Underworld, despite all the lore linking her to it throughout Greek history. She is not only a goddess of the moon, despite repeated and varied conflation with Artemis and Phoebe.

Hekate is the goddess of all of these things, and none of them. They are all transformative, changing, or encompassing a moment of change. She is transformation. She is the moment that one thing (night) becomes another (day).

And her role hasn't truly changed, despite the intervening centuries. In *The Rotting Goddess*, Jacob Rabinowitz makes a case for

Hekate being the source of the image of the Witch. She is often associated with the instruments of fate we see in Shakespeare's *Macbeth* as well as the green-skinned, death-linked hag of Hollywood's "witch," and there is truth in that, in some ways. Even among the Greeks, we can see this transformation taking place.

In Homer's *Hymn to Demeter* she is called "tender-hearted Hekate," and in the *Theogony* she is called the nurse of the young, yet in later writings she is described in darker terms. In the *Argonautica*, Apollonios Rhodes describes Hekate's approach with the words "round her horrible serpents twined themselves among the oak boughs; and there was a gleam of countless torches; and sharply howled around her the hounds of hell. All the meadows trembled at her step; and the nymphs that haunt the marsh and the river shrieked ..." [*Argonautica* 3.1212–1219] and in Euripides's *The Medea*, Hekate is Medea's matron deity. That she is linked to Medea in this way shows that, in the minds of the Greeks, she has gone from the key-bearing *kourotrophos* (child nurse) to a darker matron of witchcraft, the magic stereotypically performed by those "foreign people" (especially women). These were the Witch stereotypes of the time, and Hekate was in the thick of them.

So, we must ask ourselves, how did Hekate go from the bright-coiffed, tender-hearted goddess found in the *Hymn to Demeter* and the powerful figure offered to us in Hesiod's *Theogony*, to a dark and dangerous "witch" goddess?

Those aspects were always a part of her, in some ways, because the transformative space Hekate inhabits is not always bright or protective. The urban Greeks acknowledged that dangerous things could happen when you set foot outside your door, and Hekate was as much that transformation as she was the transformation of birth or the prosperity of the fisherman.

Hekate walked with the souls of the dead. Those souls which did not, or could not, make the journey into the Underworld were in her domain, caught forever in a transitional state between Earth and the Afterlife. They were thought to be restless, and some could possess or curse the living.

To the Greeks, magic meant a foreign ritual. Their own rituals were the domain of priests and priestesses, the ritual of the high urban temples. The rituals of the rural Greeks became seen as superstition, much like foreign ritual, and thus magic. As the years turned, the urban Greek philosophers and elite began to create their own conception of magic: theurgy, which they maintained was vastly different from the superstitious folk practices of the rural Greeks. However, the most common theurgical movement was Chaldean Theurgy, and in it she still held center stage as Hekate Soteira (savior).

Hekate's later depictions in the Chaldean Oracles speak again to her transformative nature. In the oracles Hekate is called the Cosmic Soul, the soul from which comes all other souls. She stood as the intermediary between the divine consciousness (depicted in typical Greek fashion as the "Paternal Intellect") and the earthly realm of the "Great Artisan," the shaper of the physical world. It is

through her that the material world is imbued with life, and that living beings are ensouled.

She is not only a goddess who crosses the Veil, she is the Veil. Not just between life and death, but the border between existence and oblivion. In the oracles, Hekate is again linked to the moon, another indication of her transformative nature. And given her deep connection to transformation, it's no surprise that she was so deeply connected to magic, which pulls things from mere possibility into reality, transforming it.

Modern Implications

These days, Hekate is often still seen as the goddess of witchcraft and dark magic, a dark crone, because of her connections to the line between life and death. Her chthonic roots are attributed to her aspects as a death goddess, but in truth she is not solely death aspected. Her nature is one of transformation, and though change can be terrifying and damaging, it can also be beatific. To think of her only as a chthonic, Underworld goddess is to ignore part of her nature.

These days we too often see things in terms of diametric opposites (light/dark, masculine/feminine, God/Goddess), as if the vast universe is written in binary, nothing more than ones and zeros. While these dichotomies play a role in the nature of the universe, they are also simplified depictions. Deity cannot be contained in the use of dichotomy, because deity transcends those terms.

Hekate is neither light nor dark; she is the very scale of gradation, present at the exact point at which one type of gray becomes another, between every gradient and at either end of the spectrum. Each change is her territory, and there are billions of transformations every day. We go from sleeping to waking, from hungry to full, from this place to that place. Every chemical reaction—the basis of every emotion—is a status change, and a place wherein Hekate waits.

Indeed, Pagans—used here as a catchall term—recognize that the world, that life itself, is change. Every day brings us dozens of small changes, and some days bring bigger ones. Hekate is present in our lives in innumerable ways, large and small, and through her we can learn to accept change, to accept life in all its many shades of gray.

Hekate's connection to magic is another aspect of her nature. Through magic we take what is only potential and pull it into reality, imprinting the mundane world with what could be. And this is one of the biggest changes of all, the transformation for which Hekate has always been particularly revered. Her position as the Cosmic Soul within the Chaldean Oracles speaks to the manifestation of things into reality; her connections to Medea in the Greek mind, and to magic in myriad forms, did not spring from nowhere. Magic is transformation, and it's from this that Hekate's association with it is born.

In invoking Hekate we can learn to accept changes in our lives, both positive and negative, and we can also create change in our own worlds. She aids the completion and manifestation of spells, and when called for divinatory purposes she can help to reveal the truth more readily. She can part the Veil, to allow clearer vision or communion with the dead. As *kourotrophos* (child nurse), she is a protector of children, especially when they walk hard paths, but also in the journey into adulthood.

Hekate's role as psychopomp is well known. It is she who guides Kore into and out of the Underworld on her yearly journey. That Hekate is able to come and go, and in fact to lead Kore in both directions, speaks to her nature as a crosser of boundaries.

Her likeness to the hermit of the tarot is also noteworthy: the lone figure in a dark robe, holding out a lantern (or torch) to guide the way of the traveler. Hekate protects on journeys because all journeys are transitions. Whether the road is physical or spiritual is of little consequence. She guards the crossroads, both those that line our physical reality and those that mark our passage through life, through our spirituality, and through the journey that is existence.

She is a guardian, a guide, which is something of a far cry from her depictions as a matron of dark magic. She is neither dark nor light, but like most things in nature, she is gray. Like change itself. We are refined by change; made stronger, or weaker, or brighter, or darker. We are made more clearly what we are, shown ourselves and forced to come to terms with the dark parts within us as well as the light ones. The refinement of the soul requires the changes that Hekate brings. She is a guide, a caretaker, a nurse; one who

welcomes the company of the lost spirits, who guides and protects them as they traverse the crossroads.

Night turns to day and Hekate is there, just as she is when day turns inevitably into night again. Through her the workings of the greater universe, the totality of deity, are enacted upon the world. And it is through her that we may learn to accept change, to accept the cycles of nature that are inherent in our lives.

It is therefore appropriate that she should be ever changing— that the goddess the Greeks first saw as "bright-coiffed" should in time become the "green-skinned hag," only to cycle back. All the while she is becoming something infinitely more complex and yet just the same as she has always been.

Hekate changes, and she changes us.

RESOURCES

Apollonios Rhodes. *Argonautica*. c. 250 BCE. Translated by R. C. Seaton. www.gutenberg.org/files/830/830-h/830-h.htm

Rabinowitz, Jacob. *The Rotting Goddess: The Origins of the Witch in Classical Antiquity*. New York: Autonomedia, 1996.

Marion Sipe *is a New Orleanian at heart and a traveler by nature. She has been a writer for eleven years and a practicing Witch for seventeen. A devotee of Hekate, she's served as a priestess, leading rituals with both private covens and public churches as well as teaching classes and writing on various aspects of Paganism.*

Illustrator: Tim Foley

That Old Norse Magic

Linda Raedisch

In 2003, the post office on the Faroe Islands in the Norwegian Sea issued a stamp bearing the image of a *volva*, a practitioner of the Norse brand of magic known as *seid*. Artist Anker Eli depicts the gray-haired volva striding out from the shadows of a tangled wood, staff in hand, her magic toolkit at her belt. She is every inch the proud professional.

Contrast this image with an illustration from an episode in "The History of Olav Tryggvason" in a 1932 edition of Snorre Sturlason's *Heimskringla or Lives of the Norse Kings*. The caption reads, "The wizards and troll-wise folk on

Scrat-Skerry." These *skratta*, or wizards, are also practitioners of seid. We cannot tell if their dress is rich or poor or what magical tools they might have about them because they have been bound to the *skerry*, or reef, and now the tide has come in. The pen-and-ink drawing captures them just as the sea is about to close over their heads.

Obviously, the old volva and the wizards on the skerry experienced wildly different outcomes from their practice of seid. Was it because of their sex? To answer that question, it would be helpful to start with a tidy definition of seid. Unfortunately, the literature does not offer us one. We are told that seid was originally the province of the Vanir, the old Germanic fertility gods. The practice of "witchcraft," as *seid* is often translated, was not the only stain upon the name of the Vanir; the prominent god Frey and his sister Freya, themselves the products of incest, were known to have had sexual relations with giants or trolls. According to the poem "Voluspa," it was Freya who introduced the rival clan of gods, the Aesir, to the joys of seid. She did so in the guise of a Witch called Gullveig, and she was rather a show-off about it. In the poem, Gullveig allows herself to be captured and thrown upon the hearth in Odin's hall. Three times she is burned alive and three times she emerges whole from the flames. (Did I mention they speared her too?) With the new name of Heid, meaning "shining," she goes on to teach the Aesir the intricacies of seid, including how to bewitch the minds of others. All these events take place during a formative period in the development of the world, perhaps not long after Ginnungagap, the spontaneous creation of the universe.

The Ynglinga Saga, too, credits Freya with the invention of sorcery. It also relates how readily the god Odin took to it. But there was a price to pay for proficiency at seid: it caused a man to become *ergi*. *Ergi* is a many-shaded word that can connote any or all of the following: "cowardly," "effeminate," "passively homosexual," and "versed in witchcraft." In another poem, "Lokasenna," the trickster god Loki

derides Odin for beating on a drum "as Witches do," and accuses him of being ergi.

The mention of a drum suggests that Odin was engaging in a kind of shamanism similar to that practiced by the nearby Sami (aka Lapps) and farther east by the many and sundry peoples of Siberia. It has been suggested that seid as a whole was a borrowing from the east, but things are seldom that simple. The ancient Germanic peoples (like their neighbors to the north and east) were highly animistic in their outlook, so it is natural that there would have been a healthy flow of ideas between them. While there are many impressive similarities between seid and Siberian shamanism, we should keep in mind that at one time all of Eurasia was very much like Siberia in climate and topography. They were all, ultimately, children of the same land, so it should come as no surprise to us that they practiced much the same kind of magic.

Besides, the eastern borrowing theory does not explain the stigma that was attached to the Norseman who practiced seid. To find anything akin to the Norse concept of ergi, we have to travel all the way to the Bering Strait's Chukchi Peninsula—a stretch even for the far-traveling Vikings—where we encounter the Chukchi "soft man." This was a male shaman whose personal spirits had directed him to both dress and act like a woman. Some such shamans regarded the feminine aspects of their job as just that: part of the job. Other "soft men" did indeed enter into marriages with other men in addition to keeping non-corporeal spirit-husbands. Though powerful, the "soft man," like the Norse wizard, was not held in high regard socially.

An important aspect of seid was the gaining of knowledge, both of the future in general and of the individual's fate. There is no doubt that the Norseman inhabited an uncertain world. Contrary to the stereotype of the rash Viking, he liked to test his footing before setting out on an adventure. It was perfectly acceptable to consult a volva to find out what the future held, but for a man to take up the Witch's drum himself was another matter. This is not to say that female Witches in the Old Norse sagas were immune from persecution, but when Witches are killed, it is usually in retaliation for specific crimes, most notably the aiding and abetting of their outlaw foster children.

There were a handful of men who were able to engage in all sorts of magical practices without blackening their names. These berserkers, who used the power given by Odin to make themselves invincible in battle, were sometimes considered comical but certainly never ergi. Then there were the *hamrammir*, unintentional shapeshifters whose spirits fared forth while their bodies slept. These guys were all right so long as they did not sleep through any battles. There were a few men who were suddenly overcome by sleep in the middle of the day. Upon waking, they were able to tell their fellow warriors about the distant doings of their enemies.

Unfortunately for them, the "troll-wise folk" depicted on the verge of drowning on Skrat-Skerry did not fit into any of these categories. The only specific magical act attributed to them is the conjuring of a dark mist in which to creep up on the king. Olav Tryggvason (r. 995–1000 CE), who issued this watery sentence of death, was a Christian king of Norway, his wrath fuelled by the enthusiasm of the newly converted. To him, the practice of any sort of magic was a crime. Earlier, the king had invited a host of known wizards, one Eyvind Kelda among them, to his hall at Tunsberg with the intention of burning them inside it. Eyvind escaped out the smoke hole—which suggests he had the power of flight—only to later meet his death on Skrat-Skerry.

Eyvind Kelda was the great grandson of Harald Hairfair (r. 872–930 CE), who ruled over Norway more than a hundred years before the forced Christianization of that land. Did Harald have a more sympathetic attitude toward the various types of magic at work in his realm? Not so much.

Harald had numerous wives, but it is the beautiful enchantress Snaefrid, daughter of Svasi the Finn, who concerns us here. (The saga writers used the term "Finn" to refer to any of a number of Finno-Ugric-speaking peoples, almost all of whom they credit with magical abilities.) Snaefrid bore Harald four sons, the youngest of whom was Ragnvald Rettlebone, grandfather of future-king Eyvind Kelda. Snaefrid died while still young and pretty, and her loveliness was preserved in death. Like the dwarves in "Snow White," the grieving King Harald left her laid out on the best bedclothes for three years. It wasn't until one Torliev the Wise, himself an interpreter of dreams, suggested that it was time to change the sheets underneath the corpse that its rotten condition was revealed. The body was burned straightaway and thus Snaefrid's spell over the king was broken.

Eric Bloodaxe, King Harald's son by a different mother, also married a Witch, Gunhild. Gunhild makes no bones about the fact that she had traveled to Finmark to apprentice herself to two renowned magicians. She employed the witchcraft they have taught her to escape her Finn masters, both of whom were intent on becoming her husbands. Gunhild married the indomitable Eric instead, but she never quite threw off that whiff of sorcery, eventually meeting a very witchy death by drowning in a Danish bog.

Meanwhile, Ragnvald Rettlebone, continuing in the tradition of his mother Snaefrid's side of the family, had been tutored by the wizards of Hadeland. When King Harald commanded one Vitgeir, a low-born wizard of Hordaland, to desist from his magical doings, it was Ragnvald who suffers the fallout. We are not told what sort of magic Vitgeir practices, nor to what end. Vitgeir defended himself by pointing out that Harald's own son Ragnvald was a wizard too. Forced to action, Harald sent his favorite son, Eric Bloodaxe, to make short work

of Ragnvald. Eric burned him in his hall, along with eighty other wizards.

It is stated very clearly in his saga, "King Harald did not like wizards." Presumably, he did not like Witches either, especially after that rather odd incident with Snaefrid's body. However, according to the Icelandic *Flateyjarbok*, this same King Harald was fostered by a giant of a woman named Heid. The trollish, rough-living Heid is a far cry from her "shining" namesake. Though hideous, she was a good Witch, skilled in both protective and healing magic, and King Harald held her ever in high regard. But Heid was no chaste fairy godmother. She expected sexual favors from the king's messengers in return for magical aid.

Heid is not the only such magical foster mother in Norse literature. There are others who present gifts such as stone necklaces, magic salves, and arrow-proof garments to their fosterlings. When their boys were on the lam, they hid them from their enemies. Skilled in the art of *sjonhverfing*, or "deceiving the sight," they used such tools as mist, smoke, ashes, and goat and seal skins to trick the pursuers. They could make a man disappear altogether or disguise him as a household object or animal. At first glance, these women appear to be Witches, and so the literature calls them, but they also bear a marked resemblance to the spirit-helpers of shamanic tradition. But if these wily foster mothers were originally spirits, then it would be the foster sons who are the actual wizards—an awkwardly hypocritical position indeed for the wizard-hating King Harald to find himself in!

It should not be forgotten that much insult was heaped on Freya/Gullveig/Heid for the introduction of witchcraft. Loki calls her "the foulest Witch" and accuses her of incest with her brother Frey, to whom we now turn in our search for the origins of seid. Though no accusation of ergi was ever leveled at Frey, we find some interesting things going on within his cult. In his *History of the Danes*, Saxo Grammaticus describes the "soft tinkling of bells" and effeminate dancing and some sort of ritual drama enacted within the god's sacred precinct at Uppsala. Saxo condemns all of it as wanton and unmanly.

Long before, the Roman writer Tacitus (56–117 CE) described a similar practice among the Naharvali tribe in Germany. The Naharvali worshipped twin gods known as Alcis. The Alcis' priests wore women's clothing while attending the gods' sanctuary. Tacitus equated the Alcis with Castor and Pollux, one of innumerable sets of Divine Twins found throughout the world. From Romulus and Remus to the horse-headed Asvins of the Rig Veda, these Divine Twins are invariably boys. The Asvins are still to be seen in the inward-facing horses' heads set at the gable ends of many traditional farm houses in northern Europe. Horses figured prominently in Frey's cult, so it is possible that the brother/sister duo of Frey and Freya are the result of the Indo-European version of the Divine Twins running up against an earlier

system of beliefs already at work in Scandinavia. Gradually, the Indo-European package with its new vocabulary and religion grounded in horsemanship and animal husbandry led to the masculinization of the native culture. Witchcraft became the province of the "weaker" sex, with Freya left holding the goatskin bag. But the shifting of the blame for "evil" doings was never quite complete.

One of the earliest traces of horse sacrifice occurred in what is now Lejre, Denmark. At some time during the Iron Age (c. 1200–400 BCE), a horse was slaughtered, its head and hide staked out at the edge of a pond. There is no accompanying plaque telling us that this was done in honor of Frey, but given the association of that god with horse sacrifice and the keeping of sacred horses—not to mention his reportedly horse-sized phallus!—I think it is likely.

Actually, the horse sacrifice at Lejre looks very much like what is called a *timber nid*, or "scorn pole," in the sagas. Nid was a highly ritualized form of insult, an accusation of ergi. Fail to show up for a duel and you might very well find a scorn pole erected in your dubious honor. By the Viking Age (c. 700 CE), the connection between Frey's cult and nid had been mostly forgotten, but it is still clearly a form of magic. When the volatile poet Egil Skallagrimson wished to wreak vengeance on our old friends Eric Bloodaxe and Gunhild, he cursed them by raising a hazel pole on a rocky promontory and impaling a horse's head on the end of it. Turning the dead horse's baleful gaze across the water, he invoked the land spirits against Eric. In Book Five of *The History of the Danes*, the unsavory Grep resorted to black magic after he is bested by Erik the Eloquent in a duel of words. With a "bevy of wizards" in attendance, Grep sacrifices a horse on the seashore, propping its head on the requisite pole. Eric, guessing that he is in the presence of sorcery, throws the intended curse back at the wizards. The post then falls, crushing one of the wizards to death.

Just as the raising of the scorn pole gradually devolved from sacred act to social insult, the related practice of seid may represent an ancient, sexually inclusive (or at least sexually ambiguous) aspect of the cult of Frey/Freya that was driven into the shadows by the rise of an aggressively masculine culture. Were the wizards of the medieval Scandinavian literature therefore homosexual? Like the Chukchi "soft men," no doubt some of them were and some of them were not. A few men may have turned to seid in order to gain wealth and power, but the majority of seid practitioners would not have chosen it at all; rather, it was the trollish foster mother, the spirit-husband, or spirit-wife who chose the future wizard.

To some extent, a wizard's reputation depended on which side he was on. If he set himself up against one of the heroes of the day, then he was a dark sorcerer. If he was playing for the home team, then he was just a man with useful magical talents. Another, perhaps more informative, dividing line is the use of deception. On the bright side of

seid, we have prophecy. Though time and space are manipulated, no attempt is made to deceive. On the dark side, we have *sjonh-verfing*: deceptive magic. Norse mythology makes it clear that this deceptive magic is the older of the two. How old? As old as the world itself.

Eyvind Kelda was described as "troll-wise." That is, he had access to a very deep strain of magic belonging to those trolls or giants of whom Frey was so enamored. By the nineteenth century, when the collecting of folktales began in earnest, these primordial giants had devolved into dimwitted brutes, but they were not always so. Saxo classifies the giants as the first among three classes of wizards skilled in the arts of illusion, for the giants were even older than the gods. In fact, they were the first creatures on the scene after Ginnungagap, the meeting of fire and ice from which the universe took shape.

Ginnungagap. The Dutch linguist Jan de Vries interpreted this heavily pregnant word to mean, "deceit through magic." If we are to go along with his interpretation, then Ginnungagap is the greatest illusion of all. When it comes down to it, both Eyvind Kelda and Anker Eli's volva were doing the same thing: taking active part in the ongoing beguilement that is all around us. If the world itself is an illusion, they would have reasoned, then where is the harm in tweaking it here and there to meet our own needs and the needs of our people? That is, of course, the question every Witch must ask him- or herself before entering into the practice of magic. And in that respect, not much has changed since Ginnungagap.

Resources

Blain, Jenny. *Nine Worlds of Seid-Magic: Ecstasy and Neo-shamanism in North European Paganism.* New York: Routledge, 2002.

Davidson, H. R. Ellis. *Gods and Myths of the Viking Age.* New York: Bell Publishing Company, 1981.

Hutton, Ronald. *Shamans: Siberian Spirituality in the Western Imagination.* London: Hambledon and London, 2001.

Newall, Venetia, ed. *The Witch Figure: Folklore essays by a group of scholars in England honouring the 75th birthday of Katharine M. Briggs.* Boston: Routledge and Kegan Paul, 1973.

"Norse Mythology on Stamps." Official themesite from the Faroese Philatelic Office. http://www.tjatsi.fo (accessed August 23, 2011).

"Sacrificial Bog (Iron Age)." *Sagnlandet Lejre.* http://www.sagnlandet.dk (accessed August 23, 2011).

Saxo Grammaticus. *The History of the Danes Books I-IX.* Ed. Hilda Ellis Davidson. Rochester, NY: D. S. Brewer, 1979, 1980, republished 2008.

Sturlason, Snorre. *Heimskringla or the Lives of the Norse Kings.* Ed. Erling Monsen. New York: Dover Publications, 1990.

Thorsson, Ornolfur, ed. *The Sagas of the Icelanders: A Selection.* London: Viking Penguin, 2000.

Linda Raedisch *is the author of* Night of the Witches: Folklore, Traditions and Recipes for Celebrating Walpurgis Night (*Llewellyn*). *She inhabits a modest personal library where she indulges her fascination for both Pagan survivals and the beginnings of religious and magical thought.*

Illustrator: Bri Hermanson

Look Up!
Discovering the Heavens

Susan Pesznecker

Thousands of years ago, our Stone Age ancestors looked up into the night sky with the same sense of wonder that we have today. The ancients believed that gods ruled the heavens, and they regarded heavenly occurrences—eclipses, comets, asteroid showers, moon phases—as having great significance. Archaeoastronomical monuments such as Stonehenge and the caracol at Chichén Itzá were observatories built by so-called "primitive" people to track important celestial events. Many of these alignments had accuracies of plus or minus one degree, and they still work perfectly today. And yet, none of these people had telescopes! Their only tools were their eyes, their brains, and a great deal of patience.

Later, the positions of sun and stars were used to guide navigators over land and water. Stargazing may have been the first true science, and it would one day give birth to the empiric science of astronomy. An important underlying theme of astronomy is that the universe is a rational place, with related objects that behave in predictable ways. As with any art or science, observation is both the foundation and the most important skill. And, when used in any form of study, observation is something that can be practiced, and trained.

When I work with magickal people who want to learn more about the heavens, we always begin with observation, and as you begin thinking about celestial magicks, there's no better way to start than with a night of observational skywatching. Get as far away from city lights as possible, dress warm if the weather calls for it, and take a comfortable chair and a blanket or two. If you're using a star chart, bring along a small, red LED light—red light allows you to see without affecting your night vision. Get comfortable, settle in, and look up. It's not important to name what you see—just see it. The naming can come later. Open your senses and embrace the magick. For now, the things you see will make you start asking questions: Why? Who? When? Where?

These questions will jump-start your study of celestial magicks, and eventually, as your skill grows, you'll find yourself looking at the heavens with both awe and deep respect. Whether identifying constellations, locating direction by star position, experiencing a meteor shower, or spotting one of the visible planets, you'll feel great satisfaction while constantly addressing new challenges.

Learning your way around the night sky begins with your own pair of eyes. Even today—in this era of scientific instrumentation—astronomers recommend that the night sky first be learned "by eye" before it is learned through telescopes or other tools. Step one is understanding the heavens as a giant 3D map. Imagine the night sky as a great, hollow sphere surrounding the Earth. Of course, the heavens have no known limits, but this imaginary sphere—the celestial sphere—allows us to visualize directions when we locate bodies in the night sky. To begin, imagine you're standing on Earth's north pole, then draw a line straight up, extending the pole into the heavens. You've just drawn the celestial north pole. Repeat this process for the celestial south pole. When locating stars in the night sky, the celestial poles are important reference points, and they also mark the circumpolar stars: those that never rise or set, but appear to rotate around the celestial north and south poles. Because of their fixed position in the sky, the circumpolar stars can be used to locate other stars and constellations and can also help find direction.

The current north polar star is Polaris. To find Polaris, look up and toward the north on a clear night; you'll spot it as a small, somewhat bright star. Another way to spot it is by first finding the Big Dipper. Draw an imaginary line "up" through the two stars at the non-handle side of the "dipper" (these are called the "pointer stars") and your line will run into Polaris. Mariners and travelers have long used Polaris at night to find true north. The five constellations that circle Polaris are called the north circumpolar constellations,

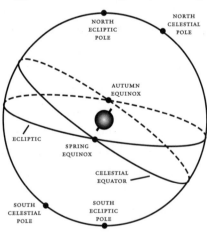

and they are visible from the Northern Hemisphere throughout the year. These are Ursa Minor (the little bear), Ursa Major (the great bear), Draco (the dragon), Cepheus (the king), and Cassiopeia (the queen). These constellations change position through the year; if you can, go out every few nights and note their position. You can identify the season by their general position and even tell time by watching their movements each night. Because they hold their relative position, they can also be used to locate other stars.

For those "down under," there's no actual south polar star. The visible star closest to the south celestial pole is the dim Sigma Octantis, sometimes called Polaris Australis. However, the bright Southern Cross (Crux) points toward the south celestial pole.

Because the pole star and circumpolar stars appear to be unchanging, they're said to have magickal properties of stability and dependability. However, due to the Earth's precession—a slow, conical wobbling—the pole stars change every several thousand years. In 2300 BCE, the north polar star was in the constellation Draco. By 12,000 CE, the star Vega in the constellation Lyra will be the north polar star, and Polaris will simply be a small circumpolar star.

You may notice that the stars appear to "twinkle." This is because they're so far away that irregularities in Earth's atmosphere make them appear to shimmer. Planets may look like stars to the naked eye, but they never appear to shimmer or twinkle, as they're much closer to us than stars and not subject to atmospheric effects.

Now, imagine you're standing on Earth's equator. Imagine extending the entire equator outward into the heavens and you create the celestial equator, another important heavenly marker. The celestial equator marks the boundary between the Northern and Southern Hemispheres. However, note that it doesn't mark the sun's path. The apparent yearly path of the sun through the stars and around the celestial sphere is called the ecliptic or solar ecliptic. This circular path is actually tilted 23.5 degrees off the celestial equator. Because Earth's rotational axis is tilted by 23.5 degrees with respect to its orbital plane, its relationship to the ecliptic is also tilted.

The ecliptic and celestial equator do intersect at two points. When the sun crosses one of these intersecting points, the vernal (spring) equinox or autumnal (fall) equinox occurs. At these points, the sun is halfway through its annual trip around the ecliptic; when it crosses the celestial equator, day and night at the equator are approximately equal in length.

To measure distances in the celestial sphere, we use degrees and angles. Why? Because expressing position in degrees can help one locate a heavenly object or point an object out to another viewer. There are 360 degrees in a full circle and 90 degrees in a right angle. Any object directly overhead is 90 degrees above the horizon and is said to be at zenith. An object "half-way up" in the sky (i.e., an equal distance between the horizon and zenith) is about 45 degrees above the horizon.

In measuring smaller angles, you have the perfect tool close by: your hand! The average adult human hand—held at arm's length—provides a great way to estimate angles. A closed fist covers an angle of about 10 degrees, while your widest finger is about 1 degree. In

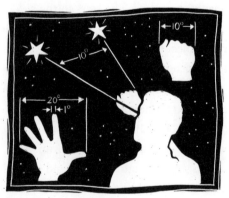

other words, two stars that are one fist apart are about 10 degrees apart, and if they're about halfway up between the horizon and zenith, they are at about 45 degrees relative to the horizon. Spread out your entire hand and the distance from the tip of little finger to the tip of your thumb is about 20 degrees.

Picture yourself back out in the dark, away from city lights. If you lie down on your back and watch the stars for the entire night, they'll appear to rise from the east and set, dropping below the horizon, in the west. To us, the stars appear to move quite rapidly. But in reality, we're doing most of the moving, and the star's apparent "motion" is a result of Earth's rotation. Earth rotates continuously from west to east, making a complete rotation every twenty-four hours and creating the cycle of day and night. Because of this, the sun, moon, and stars always appear to rise in the east, set in the west, and move through the sky over the course of twelve hours. At any given moment, it's daytime (light) on half of Earth and nighttime (dark) on the other half.

The constellations visible in the night sky also appear to change position over the course of a year. This is because in addition to its rotation, Earth also orbits the sun. Different parts of Earth thus face different parts of the heavens, presenting us with changing (but predictable) views of the stars. And the stars move, too! Stars belong to galaxies, and galaxies rotate continuously; so, all stars are in continuous motion. A few million years from now, the night sky—seen from Earth—will look completely different.

Step outside, look up into the night sky, and know that what you're seeing never fails to be wondrous or unique. The night sky is full of magick. If you aren't amazed by what's wheeling by overhead, you're not paying attention.

Susan Pesznecker's *full bio appears on page 47.*

Illustrator: Kathleen Edwards

Gender-Bending & Transcending

Melanie Marquis

We are energy born into bodies, each spirit resonating its unique vibrations throughout and beyond the flesh. Our form the instrument, our soul the song; the ways we choose to dance to the music of our own lives is an artist's choice—will you live the masterpiece you sense inside you, or will you let yourself be limited to a predetermined script? Whether you are heterosexual, homosexual, bisexual, transgendered, or anywhere in between, we all can benefit from moving beyond the place of identifying solely with the bodies we are occupying. The feminine and the masculine coexist; there is a polarity, yes, but a polarity in which there is plenty of middle ground where the two shall meet. From the Goddess to the God, from the God to the Goddess, life's rhythm is an interaction of opposite forces, a push and pull of meshing energies that work together as a whole, never truly separated. The Witch who wants to deeply delve into the mysteries of sex

From the Goddess to the God, from the God to the Goddess, life's rhythm is an interaction of opposite forces, a push and pull of meshing energies that work together as a whole, never truly separated.

and the soul will gain great insights from challenging, questioning, and transcending the body's idea of itself and its limits through special arts of magick and ritual.

Curious? There are many ways to explore spirituality beyond the body. From gender-bending rituals to magick transcendent of any gender-based restrictions, experimenting safely in a way that feels comfortable to you will help you break through your boundaries. The benefits of such exercises are unique to each Witch, but one thing is certain: gender-bending and transcending through magick and ritual will help you gain intricate and intimate knowledge of yourself and the Divine, and as a result, your understanding of the Craft is sure to grow.

Gender-bending rituals have many useful applications. From dissolving limitations or negative beliefs imposed by oneself or others to better accessing and utilizing specific energies and archetypes to use in spellwork, switching mentally to a new gender for the space of a ritual can be undertaken to fulfill a variety of magickal and spiritual purposes. For example, suppose you want to experience a Dianic ritual, but you happen to have a penis. Through specific ritual techniques, you can more fully embrace your inner female and allow your spirit and your magick to easily overcome any outward physical manifestations to the contrary. As another example, imagine you are a very masculine man who wants to work a spell for nourishing, a characteristic you personally have associated with femininity. In this case, a gender-bending ritual might be just the thing to put you more in touch with the Divine Feminine energies within you, enabling you to better work the magick at hand. Whatever the particular purpose of the ritual, there are gender-bending techniques that can be adjusted and adapted to suit your goals as well as your comfort zone. Here are some ideas to help you craft a ceremony that's just right for you.

You'll need to first choose the energies with which you wish to work. This is the power source that acts as primary or supplementary fuel for your magickal ceremony. For a gender-bending ritual, consider calling on a deity or deities of the gender you wish to experience. Or, choose a hermaphroditic godform with both male and female characteristics. You can also connect with lunar and solar energies to help you with your gender-bending ritual: call on the moon to enhance femininity, or summon the sun to enhance masculine qualities. Consider wearing symbols of the deities or energies you wish to have present and decorate your altar with associated objects, stones, and herbs. Cross-dressing and the use of cosmetics can further increase the power of the ritual.

Take some time to clear your head, then think about your ritual's purpose. What do you hope to achieve? What would you like to experience? Will the gender-bending ritual go against your core desires, or is this switch a reflection of your true feelings about who you are? Having an idea of where you're aiming to go will do much

to get you there, ensuring an enriching, satisfying, and effective experience. Next, sense the energies within your body while at the same time becoming aware of the energies outside of you, surrounding you and all that is. Incorporate meditations, music, and visualizations if you like, to put you in a mood for magick.

When it comes time to clear the space and cast the circle, you might consider giving your typical techniques a twist. Pine cones, swords, and long rectangular stones can be incorporated for masculine themed rituals; apricots, cups, and triangular or round stones for rituals with a feminine theme.

Use your usual methods to evoke or invoke any energies or entities you wish to be present, only add in to your words or actions a clear expression of your ritual's intent. For example, if you are invoking Cernunnos in order to experience a masculine identity, tell the god exactly why you wish to do this.

The heart of the ritual is individualized to its purpose, and the actions and mental processes you undertake in this stage of the magickal ceremony are of your own design. Here, what you want determines what you do. For example, if you are physically and/or spiritually male or hermaphroditic and wish to get in touch with feminine energies, you might touch yourself while imagining your body as a woman's body, letting the pleasure flow through you softly. As your arousal builds, you might hold some of the energy in your breasts and genitals, concentrating and magnifying the power in these areas until you can expand the energy and mentally create a new energetic form surrounding you, a type of aura body that matches the gender identity you are seeking to experience. Likewise, if you are physically female but you don't identify with feminine energies and would like to connect more with your inner goddess, you might touch yourself as if you were that goddess, envisioning these feminine energies entering into you through your pleasured flesh. As another example, if you wish to experience a hermaphroditic identity, you might masturbate while switching your mental imagery, alternating between seeing your body as female and as male.

Perhaps you don't want to emphasize any particular feminine, masculine, or hermaphroditic qualities, but instead you wish to overcome and transcend altogether any boundaries or limits placed on us by the inner or outer manifestations of gender. In this case, you might consider evoking or invoking a genderless deity or elemental energy at the start of the ritual, then proceeding to notice, examine, and release any gendered qualities remaining within you. You might visualize yourself alternating between different genders, transforming outwardly yet inwardly unchanged. Feel yourself as part of something larger than the physical body; notice how your sexuality is far beyond the constraints of mundane conformity, but is instead ever-present and ever-changing.

Experiencing a different gender identity can broaden your perspective and widen the base of your spiritual understanding. Consider taking time at this stage of the ritual to contemplate any problems, challenges, or spiritual questions you are currently facing, seeing the issue with new insight brought on by the adjustment to your usual inner or outer identity.

Whatever particular form it may take, once the core of the ritual proceedings is complete, cut through any visualizations you used to make changes to your energetic body, just as you cut the circle at the end of a rite to release the energies called forth. If, on the other hand, you are going for a more permanent transformation of gendered qualities, keep the energetic facade you've built through the ritual, imagining your own body truly fusing with the new identity.

When it comes to gender-bending rituals, the possibilities are endless, the crossover potential unlimited. Try a little gender-bending or transcending to give your typical rituals a twist; add an extra splash of femininity or masculinity to your soul before meditations, magick, and holy rites to gain new perspectives and build your versatility and spiritual understanding as a Witch. For a group rite, try switching roles, the priest becoming the priestess and vice versa. For solitaries, consider trying out a whole moon cycle of gender-bending rituals, experiencing what it's like to emphasize masculinity, femininity, and dual sexuality in turn, keeping a journal of your impressions after each ceremony for further examination and contemplation. You can even use gender-bending magick in more playful ways—put on a new extra masculine or feminine facade before going out to meet that special someone, try mentally switching to a different gender to bust through creative blocks, or let go of gender altogether to transcend social masks and constraints anytime you're feeling nervous or out of place. Whether for magickal reasons, for spiritual purposes, or simply to have fun and try something new, gender-bending rituals can open up a world of options for the creative and free-thinking Witch.

Melanie Marquis's *full bio appears on page 119.*

Illustrator: Christa Marquez

Experiencing the
Aura Evolution

Kala Ambrose

I n early 2001, I began sharing with
my students my impression that
there would be a difficult period of
time coming. The energy would feel
thick, heavy, and dark, and finding
the energy to conduct light work and
spiritual training would feel more challenging. I shared that the most difficult
time would be during 2007 through
2014, as this time would test people
down to their core beliefs, morals, and
values, including their sense of self and
their personal strength to endure what
they see going on around them in the
world. Many people are experiencing

*This article is derived from
Kala Ambrose's book
The Awakened Aura,
published in 2011 by
Llewellyn Publications.*

this difficulty right now, as it simply feels harder to do things they previously did with ease on a daily basis.

Part of the vibrational energy that I speak of is coming from the ethers—the etheric realms and beyond—and is causing an effect at this time that is felt by all things on Earth. This ether resonates in our auric bodies and in nature. We are in a period of rapid evolution. In order to evolve, we first must cleanse and purify our surroundings and ourselves energetically. In a very basic example, I describe the concept of a junk closet in the home. In this closet are lots of things that we use often, yet no one wants to take the time to clean out the closet, go through what we no longer need, discard it, and reorganize the items. We are so caught up in our daily activities that we avoid taking the time to clean out the closet. Our minds are so busy that we are unable to see that cleaning it out would actually give us more time in our daily life, since we wouldn't waste time pulling out half of the junk in the closet to find the one thing we are looking for on a given day. Instead, we allow the clutter to grow in the closet, convincing ourselves that we don't have the time to deal with the problem. One day, the clutter becomes so great that we can no longer shove anything else inside, and when we open the door, the enormity of the mass of things falls upon us.

In the same way, our auric fields are storage containers, our "closets," and they can hold the great amount of energy we place inside of them. For many lifetimes now, we have been able to continue to place more emotional and mental baggage as well as old karmic debt into these fields and sort through them as we choose. We have chosen to keep stuffing things into the fields, deciding we'll deal with them on another day. With the new age coming from the Divine Feminine, the Great Mother is saying that we cannot continue as we have been and it's time to clean house. In a grand cosmic way, we cannot move forward and go outside of our lower auric fields to play until we have cleaned our closet (our auric fields).

We are being provided with tools in our aura to help us accomplish this work, and the effects of this evolution are being felt by all beings, elements, and elementals on Earth.

Where We're Heading

Our future has science and spirituality working together to unravel the mysteries of the Universe. Spiritual mystics have shared universal truths since ancient times, and now the general consciousness of humanity is open to receiving this knowledge. This knowledge becomes available to us not only in the mental field, but as we shift from the third dimension into the fourth and fifth dimensions, we will receive and understand information through all of the auric fields on a greater scale. During this new age of enlightenment in which we are living, science is beginning to catch on to what the mystics have been teaching for centuries and is discovering tangible ways to study these teachings through quantum physics.

When we look at our soul and the auric fields, as they fully exist, they extend far beyond the seven planes closest around the body. The "As Above, So Below" hermetic axiom can best be used to liken the auric fields to the shape of an upside-down pyramid. The pyramid's large base is up in the spiritual planes, where souls go when they leave the earthly plane. The tiny capstone (tip) of the pyramid is the section that resides within your body, in the heart. This capstone contains the spark of life, the life force that activates the soul and begins to pour all that is you from the higher planes down into your heart when you are born.

As you can imagine, this is a lot of energy and information to absorb, so the process slows as the pyramid grows narrower until it reaches the tip inside of you. This capstone has a crystalline structure that captures all of the experiences in your life, returns this energy information back up to the higher planes, and stores these experiences in the akashic records.

From this capstone, a second pyramid is generated right-side up, which encapsulates the auric fields around our body down to the ground. The two pyramids interconnect at each capstone in the heart and are joined through the energy cords and meridians throughout the body. This ancient teaching has been symbolized in many forms, including the Star of David, the tetrahedron, and the Flower of Life.

Here on the earthly plane, we currently ground through the lower chakras. We tend to think of the spiritual planes as places above us in the sky. There are many levels to the higher planes, but they can be reached from various points of your body, including your heart, throat, and third-eye region. The higher planes are more accessible than most people realize. In the higher planes, the confining rules of the earthly plane do not exist, including the limitations of time as well as the concept of being in one space at one time. The higher one moves into the spiritual planes, the greater the ability to be omnipresent. This allows us, basically, to be in several places at once. The first plane where this ability appears is in the astral field.

As we take this big-picture look at the auric fields, we see that the majority of the essence and energy of what makes us who we are resides in the higher planes, and that only a small portion of that energy trickles down into the body. The majority of our essence and soul energy remains in the higher planes with a much greater consciousness and awareness, making up the sum of all of our parts, lifetimes, and experiences.

When we reach out to speak to a loved one who has passed on, we connect with this part of their essence, what we would refer to as their Higher Self. The Higher Self retains memory of all lifetimes, including the energy of who this person was in the lifetime we remember them from. This aspect of the person then appears to us in their energetic form with access to all the memories and experiences from this lifetime.

The Evolution of the Auric Fields

Since 1999, I've observed new crystalline structures forming in the aura that I have never seen in the human aura field before. It appears that our spiritual bodies are evolving at a rapid pace that could

be referred to as a "quickening," and our energy bodies are being attuned right before our very eyes. Our energy bodies are being reconstructed and are opening up to allow more light and energy to flow through us than ever before.

These structures are creating new energy cords, which form a grid around the auric body. Beginning in 2006, I began to observe these cords connecting, expanding, and vibrating in the auric fields of many people with significantly greater energy. The grid and the cord connection are highly conscious and interactive. They respond to conscious contact both from the individual who is aware of this new field around them and from others who engage in communication with the cords on an intuitive level.

The cords connect in three places inside the body: the solar plexus chakra, the heart chakra, and above the head. The area above the head does not interact directly with the crown chakra; it is connected with the higher planes, where information and light flows directly into the aura, which is the eighth chakra. The completed grid shape has cords of light extending from the chakras into the newly formed grid around the body.

The three main cords expand and connect with smaller cords coming from each of the other chakras and from the internal organs. They connect to the grid and then extend farther outward to connect with cords coming from the higher levels of the energy bodies and beyond. These cords then extend their connections outward. Each cord has to "grow," and when a cord grows long enough to reach the other cords, it "snaps together," creating a new grid system around the person.

I refer to this new structure as the "higher consciousness grid," and the speed at which it is evolving is fascinating. Each time I view one of these almost fully formed grids on someone I'm reading, I see more neuronlike networks connecting into the grid. The structures are expanding the auric field, from the old form of the oval shape around the body into a more expansive grid system connected by the cords. The cords are able to stretch and grow and have tendrils, which can reach out to create new patterns. It appears to me to be a much stronger system, with the cords forming the grid, and light and energy running through the cords at a much faster rate than the old auric fields.

Intuitively, it feels as if our consciousness is being gathered through these cords and a ship is being created around each of us to transport our consciousness and essence to a different place.

If there was ever a time I wondered about how we would manage to shift from the third dimension into the fourth and fifth, I no longer have any of those concerns, as I see the actual energetic transportation devices being built around people every day in preparation for this evolution.

The consciousness grids—or "ships," as I call them—vary in size and strength. The most fully formed grids I have seen are emerging from people who emit the strongest energy from their heart chakra area. These grids, which are able to fully extend from the heart chakra, form a strong, double-walled oval shape around the body, with a malleable texture and beautiful glow. These structures pulse with energy and a vibrant light. The colors of the aura can be seen through this grid and there are new colors coming from the interior of these cords.

The heart chakra grid is one of several types of grid structures being formed in the auric field. Some people are not quite ready to open their heart chakra to the point of this energetic vibration. In these cases, grid systems are formed using a complex system of connections that run through the three lower chakras. The colors and sizes of these cords vary accordingly. For those who are not quite ready to move from the solar plexus chakra into the heart chakra energetic level, the grid appears to be shaping the new body of each person using the solar plexus chakra as the base point.

This transition is creating an energetic transformation in the person. It is significant and similar to what the ancient Egyptians referred to as the power of the light body to do "magic" in order for humanity to evolve into light beings.

What's Coming in the New Decade

This new decade brings a major shift to the masses in regard to conscious thinking and opens the door to further self-realization and heightened psychic awareness and abilities.

Time has been moving at an unparalleled rate, which thus far in the twenty-first century has brought us the gift of seeing our hopes, dreams, thoughts, and wishes manifest at a surprising and sometimes alarming rate. Truly this current decade has focused on manifesting the belief that *if we can think it, we can achieve it.*

As we've dared to dream and open our minds, the shift of ages from Pisces to Aquarius is gifting us with a never-before-seen outpouring of information. No longer are we reliant upon a particular university, library, or reference text to provide information. From the spiritual planes above, Aquarius has tipped the waters of illumination and knowledge from the gods back down to Earth for us to receive. Thanks to the air sign of Aquarius, we have seen this information fly quickly through the Internet, connecting humanity on a global scale and providing information on any topic we can conceive of, at any time, with multiple resources to consider and cross-reference. With this gift of knowledge in the new millennium, we've shared our life stories, bonded in social networks, blogged our thoughts, shopped at and supported local and global businesses whose storefronts we may never see in person, learned about

cultures throughout the world, and tweeted our thoughts to thousands just as quickly as we think them.

What will the next decade bring? We are being set free in body, mind, and spirit to release karmic ties and bindings and operate from our higher energy bodies. The bridge between the lower and higher auric fields is open, and we can operate from our astral field with greater ease and expand our psychic abilities.

Beginning in 2020, the journey evolves as we move from knowledge into wisdom. What is the big difference between knowledge and wisdom? Knowledge is the awareness of information. Wisdom is gained from taking the knowledge, putting it into action, observing how the action causes various reactions, and then gaining discernment of how it best can be used. A person may be knowledgeable without being wise. Humanity must develop discernment in order to become wise.

We are moving into a new Age of Enlightenment. The Aquarian information from the gods can no longer be contained, the Divine

Feminine is being released in all her glory, and we will once again see a Renaissance period, where great art, architecture, philosophy, literature, and science will develop and flourish. During this decade, the greatest minds will stir to share, to illuminate, and to build and create works and ideas that will be admired around the world.

If you have been wondering "*When is my time?*"—2020 is your destiny date. In this coming decade, we will connect mind, body, and spirit as the ancients did, connecting with our muses, using our intuition to guide us, and working in tandem on the spiritual and earthly planes.

It's here, we're here, and this coming decade will be history-making on every level.

Noted wisdom teacher, author, intuitive, inspirational speaker, and host of the "Explore Your Spirit with Kala Radio and TV Show" (www.Explore YourSpirit.com), **Kala Ambrose**'s *teachings are described as discerning, empowering, and inspiring. Whether she's speaking with world-renowned experts on her show, writing about empowering lifestyle choices, reporting on new discoveries in the scientific and spiritual arenas, or teaching to groups around the country, fans around the world tune in daily for her inspirational musings and lively, thought-provoking conversations. Kala Ambrose is the author of three books, including the award-winning* 9 Life Altering Lessons (Reality Press), Ghosthunting North Carolina (Clerisy Press), *and* The Awakened Aura (Llewellyn). *A highly interactive teacher on a mission to educate, entertain, and inspire, Kala writes for the* Huffington Post *and presents workshops nationally on the Mind/Body/ Spirit connection, including Auras and Energy Fields, Developing Business Intuition, and Wisdom Teachings at the Omega Institute, the Learning Annex, LilyDale Assembly, and online in presentations including John Edward's InfiniteQuest and Daily Om.*

Illustrator: Rik Olson

The Lunar Calendar

September 2012 to December 2013

SEPTEMBER

S	M	T	W	T	F	S
						1
2	3	4	5	6	7	8
9	10	11	12	13	14	15
16	17	18	19	20	21	22
23	24	25	26	27	28	29
30						

OCTOBER

S	M	T	W	T	F	S
	1	2	3	4	5	6
7	8	9	10	11	12	13
14	15	16	17	18	19	20
21	22	23	24	25	26	27
28	29	30	31			

NOVEMBER

S	M	T	W	T	F	S
				1	2	3
4	5	6	7	8	9	10
11	12	13	14	15	16	17
18	19	20	21	22	23	24
25	26	27	28	29	30	

DECEMBER

S	M	T	W	T	F	S
						1
2	3	4	5	6	7	8
9	10	11	12	13	14	15
16	17	18	19	20	21	22
23	24	25	26	27	28	29
30	31					

2013

JANUARY

S	M	T	W	T	F	S
		1	2	3	4	5
6	7	8	9	10	11	12
13	14	15	16	17	18	19
20	21	22	23	24	25	26
27	28	29	30	31		

FEBRUARY

S	M	T	W	T	F	S
					1	2
3	4	5	6	7	8	9
10	11	12	13	14	15	16
17	18	19	20	21	22	23
24	25	26	27	28		

MARCH

S	M	T	W	T	F	S
					1	2
3	4	5	6	7	8	9
10	11	12	13	14	15	16
17	18	19	20	21	22	23
24	25	26	27	28	29	30
31						

APRIL

S	M	T	W	T	F	S
	1	2	3	4	5	6
7	8	9	10	11	12	13
14	15	16	17	18	19	20
21	22	23	24	25	26	27
28	29	30				

MAY

S	M	T	W	T	F	S
			1	2	3	4
5	6	7	8	9	10	11
12	13	14	15	16	17	18
19	20	21	22	23	24	25
26	27	28	29	30	31	

JUNE

S	M	T	W	T	F	S
						1
2	3	4	5	6	7	8
9	10	11	12	13	14	15
16	17	18	19	20	21	22
23	24	25	26	27	28	29
30						

JULY

S	M	T	W	T	F	S
	1	2	3	4	5	6
7	8	9	10	11	12	13
14	15	16	17	18	19	20
21	22	23	24	25	26	27
28	29	30	31			

AUGUST

S	M	T	W	T	F	S
				1	2	3
4	5	6	7	8	9	10
11	12	13	14	15	16	17
18	19	20	21	22	23	24
25	26	27	28	29	30	31

SEPTEMBER

S	M	T	W	T	F	S
1	2	3	4	5	6	7
8	9	10	11	12	13	14
15	16	17	18	19	20	21
22	23	24	25	26	27	28
29	30					

OCTOBER

S	M	T	W	T	F	S
		1	2	3	4	5
6	7	8	9	10	11	12
13	14	15	16	17	18	19
20	21	22	23	24	25	26
27	28	29	30	31		

NOVEMBER

S	M	T	W	T	F	S
					1	2
3	4	5	6	7	8	9
10	11	12	13	14	15	16
17	18	19	20	21	22	23
24	25	26	27	28	29	30

DECEMBER

S	M	T	W	T	F	S
1	2	3	4	5	6	7
8	9	10	11	12	13	14
15	16	17	18	19	20	21
22	23	24	25	26	27	28
29	30	31				

Thirteen Classic Witch Movies
Every Witch Should See

Magenta

Witches on the silver screen range from beautiful and alluring to grotesque and dangerous to frumpy and bumbling. On the following pages are thirteen movies with Witches as main characters that I recommend to any Witch. Some are serious, some are funny. Grab some popcorn and relax for an evening, or plan a group viewing so you can discuss the portrayal of Witches with your coven (sample discussion questions follow the movie profiles). Most of these movies are readily available—try your local library, a mail-in DVD service (such as Netflix), or a used bookstore. These films portray Witches in all kinds of ways, with varying degrees of accuracy and humor. Don't believe what you see at the movies, though—Witches are far more complicated than any one story.

Magenta Griffith *has been a Witch for more than thirty years and a High Priestess for more than twenty years. She is a founding member of the coven Prodea, which has been celebrating rituals since 1980. She is also a member of various Pagan organizations, such as Covenant of the Goddess. She presents classes and workshops at a variety of events around the Midwest. She shares her home with a small black cat and a large collection of books.*

2012
SEPTEMBER

SU	M	TU	W	TH	F	SA
						1
2	3 Labor Day	4	5	6	7	8
9	10	11	12	13	14	15 ● 10:11 p
16	17	18	19	20	21 UN International Day of Peace	22 Mabon/ Fall Equinox
23	24	25	26	27	28	29 ☺ Harvest Moon, 11:19 p
30						

New and Full Moon dates are shown in Eastern Time. You must adjust
the time (and date) for your time zone.

Hocus Pocus (1993)

Three hundred years, ago in Salem, Massachusetts, a boy named Thackery Binx was turned into a black cat, and consequently, the three Sanderson sisters were hung as Witches. Now, on Halloween, three teenagers leave a Halloween party so they can explore the Sanderson sisters' abandoned cottage, which has been turned into a museum. They hear the story of the Black Flamed Candle, which will bring the Witches back when lit. One teen laughs at the idea and lights the candle, and the three sisters appear (aided by spectacular effects): Winnie (Bette Midler), Sarah (Sarah Jessica Parker), and Mary (Kathy Najimy). Naturally, they want to stay alive and need the life force of little children to do so. Binx, the black cat, helps the teens escape, and the chase continues all night and all over town.

LENGTH: 96 minutes
RATING: PG

2012
OCTOBER

SU	M	TU	W	TH	F	SA
	1	2	3	4	5	6
7	8 *Columbus Day (observed)*	9	10	11	12	13
14	15 ● 8:02 a	16	17	18	19	20
21	22	23	24	25	26	27
28	29 ☺ *Blood Moon, 3:49 p*	30	31 *Samhain/ Halloween*			

MOVIE QUOTE:
Dani: It's a full moon tonight. That's when all the weirdos are out.

Cast a Deadly Spell (1991)

This noir/horror crossover is unusual in both setting and background. In this fantasy version of 1940s Los Angeles, magic is real, monsters and mythical beasts stalk the back alleys, and zombies are used as cheap labor. Hardboiled private detective Phillip Lovecraft (Fred Ward) is hired by a mysterious millionaire to investigate the theft of an unusual book, the *Necronomicon*. He learns the book in question holds the key to bringing back the "Old Ones" and taking over the world. And the millionaire's daughter has disappeared—is she alive or dead? Can he find the book, and the girl, before she is sacrificed to summon unthinkable horrors?

LENGTH: 96 minutes
RATING: R

SU	M	TU	W	TH	F	SA
				1 *All Saints' Day*	2	3
4 *DST ends, 2 a*	5	6 *Election Day (general)*	7	8	9	10
11 *Veterans Day*	12	13　● 5:08 p *Solar eclipse*	14	15	16	17
18	19	20	21	22 *Thanksgiving Day*	23	24
25	26	27	28　☺ *Lunar eclipse Mourning Moon, 9:46 a*	29	30	

MOVIE QUOTE:
Lovecraft: Magic is the way of the future. Wouldn't want to buck the future,
would you, Bradbury?

Kiki's Delivery Service (1989)

In this classic animated film by Hayao Miyazaki, it's traditional for Witches to live alone for a year at the age of thirteen. Kiki takes off for the big city with her best friend Jiji, a talkative black cat, and settles in Koriko, a beautiful city by the sea. Kiki finds friends and a place to stay. She has one unique Witch's skill: her ability to fly on a broom. And so Kiki starts an air delivery service. She must cope with her independence, and the usual—and not-so-usual—adolescent difficulties.

LENGTH: 103 minutes
RATING: G

2012
DECEMBER

SU	M	TU	W	TH	F	SA
						1
2	3	4	5	6	7	8
9	10	11	12	13 ● 3:42 a	14	15
16	17	18	19	20	21 Yule/ Winter Solstice	22
23	24 Christmas Eve	25 Christmas Day	26	27	28 ☺ Long Night's Moon, 5:21 a	29
30	31 New Year's Eve					

MOVIE QUOTE:
Jiji: You'd think they'd never seen a girl and a cat on a broom before.

The Witches of Eastwick (1987)

Three best friends, previously married but now single—sculptress Alex (Cher), cellist Jane (Susan Sarandon), and writer Sukie (Michelle Pfeiffer)—are feeling emotionally and sexually repressed, in large part due to living in the small New England town of Eastwick. After their latest conversation lamenting the lack of suitable local men, mysterious Daryl Van Horne (Jack Nicholson, in one of his best roles) arrives in town. Despite being vulgar, crude, brazen, and not particularly handsome, Daryl manages to seduce each woman, and the three women blossom emotionally and sexually. They soon realize they are in his power, and that Daryl is far more than he appeared to be. The three decide to experiment with some talents learned indirectly from Daryl to get back control of their lives. Based on the novel by John Updike.

LENGTH: 118 minutes

RATING: R

2013
JANUARY

SU	M	TU	W	TH	F	SA
		I New Year's Day	2	3	4	5
6	7	8	9	10	11 ● 2:44 p	12
13	14	15	16	17	18	19
20	21 Martin Luther King, Jr. Day	22	23	24	25	26 ☺ 11:38 p Cold Moon
27	28	29	30	31		

MOVIE QUOTE:
Daryl: It's women who are the source ... the only power. Nature, birth, rebirth.

The Wicker Man (1973)

Police Sergeant Neil Howie (Edward Woodward) arrives on a remote Scottish island looking for a missing teenager girl, Rowan Morrison. Howie shows a photo of the missing girl to the locals, but they deny she exists. He meets Lord Summerisle (Christopher Lee), owner of the island, famous for its apples and other fruits, who explains that they are all practicing Pagans. Howie observes the islanders' Pagan customs with increasing alarm. He thinks Rowan is alive but the villagers are preparing to sacrifice her to make the apples grow. However, the situation is not what it seems to be, and Howie's persistence proves his undoing. Don't bother with the 2006 remake of this movie; I can only recommend the 1973 version.

LENGTH: 88 minutes
RATING: R

2013
FEBRUARY

SU	M	TU	W	TH	F	SA
					1	2 *Imbolc/ Groundhog Day*
3	4	5	6	7	8	9
10 ● 2:20 a	11	12	13	14 *Valentine's Day*	15	16
17	18 *Presidents' Day*	19	20	21	22	23
24	25 ☺ *Quickening Moon, 3:26 p*	26	27	28		

MOVIE QUOTE:
May Morrison: You'll simply never understand the true nature of sacrifice.

Simon, King of the Witches (1971)

Simon Sinestrari (Andrew Prine), a cynical ceremonial magician, sells charms and potions for money while on a quest to become a god. Turk, a young male prostitute, befriends him, and introduces Simon to his world of drugs and wild parties. Turk and Simon crash a "Wiccan" ceremony presided over by a priestess (Ultra Violet). Every cliché in the book is dragged out: spooky music, sinister chants, references to "The Queen of the Night," naked people and, eventually, worship of a live goat. Simon is unimpressed with the goings-on and eventually ridicules the coven; he must leave in a hurry with the angry coven on his tail. What sets this movie apart from other occult films of its time is that the script is far more knowledgeable about the esoteric than most.

LENGTH: 99 minutes
RATING: R

2013
MARCH

SU	M	TU	W	TH	F	SA
					1	2
3	4	5	6	7	8	9
10 DST begins, 2 a	11 ● 3:51 p	12	13	14	15	16
17 St. Patrick's Day	18	19	20 Ostara/ Spring Equinox	21	22	23
24	25	26	27 ☺ Storm Moon, 5:27 a	28	29	30
31						

MOVIE QUOTE:
Simon: My boy, you don't know how important it is for a magician
to have the right kind of workshop.

Bedknobs and Broomsticks (1971)

During WWII in England, three children are sent to live with Eglantine Price (Angela Lansbury), an apprentice Witch. They find out about her witchcraft and blackmail her: to keep her secret, she must give them something magical. She takes a knob from her bed and places the "famous magic traveling spell" on it. The four of them use the enchanted bedknob to travel to London, where they meet Emelius Browne, headmaster of Miss Price's witchcraft correspondence school. Miss Price tells him her plan to find the substitutiary locomotion spell, which brings inanimate objects to life. After many adventures, they find the necessary words in a book, and Miss Price attempts the spell but is unable to control it. That night, a German raiding party invades and takes over Miss Price's house. They are captured and taken to the village museum inside the old castle. Mr. Browne suggests Miss Price cast the substitutiary locomotion spell on the old uniforms and weapons in the castle. She uses the spell to create a magical army of medieval knights, Elizabethan Guards, Cavaliers, Redcoats, and Highlanders that then defeat the Germans.

LENGTH: 117 minutes
RATING: G

2013
APRIL

SU	M	TU	W	TH	F	SA
	1 All Fools' Day	2	3	4	5	6
7	8	9	10 ● 5:35 a	11	12	13
14	15	16	17	18	19	20
21	22 Earth Day	23	24	25 ☺ Lunar eclipse Wind Moon, 3:57 P	26	27
28	29	30				

MOVIE QUOTE:
Bear: People? People? Oh, no! What scurvy luck!

TAURUS

Rosemary's Baby (1968)

A young couple, Guy (John Cassavettes) and Rosemary (Mia Farrow), move into a new apartment, only to be surrounded by peculiar neighbors and occurrences. Their next-door neighbors, the Castevets, take an unnatural interest in both of them. After Guy and Rosemary plan to have a baby, she has a strange interlude, dreaming or imagining she had sex with a monster in front of a group of people. She soon finds she is pregnant, and consults Dr. Sapirstein, an obstetrician recommended by the Castevets. Instead of vitamins, Sapirstein prescribes a tonic prepared by Minnie Castevet. Rosemary loses weight and is sick most of the time. She is convinced that something is wrong, but no one will believe her. Based on the novel by Ira Levin.

LENGTH: 136 minutes
RATING: R

2013
MAY

SU	M	TU	W	TH	F	SA
			1	2	3	4
				Beltane		
5	6	7	8	9 ● 8:28 p	10	11
				Solar eclipse		
12	13	14	15	16	17	18
Mother's Day						
19	20	21	22	23	24	25 ☺
						Lunar eclipse *Flower Moon,* 12:25 a
26	27	28	29	30	31	
	Memorial Day *(observed)*					

MOVIE QUOTE:
Minnie: He chose you, honey! From all the women in the world,
to be the mother of his only living son!

Burn, Witch, Burn (1962)

Norman Taylor (Peter Wyngarde), a skeptical psychology professor lecturing on belief and superstition, discovers that his wife, Tansy, has been practicing witchcraft for years. She insists that her charms have been responsible for his academic success and his well-being. A firm rationalist and angry at her superstition, Taylor makes her burn all magical objects in the house, and things start to go wrong almost immediately. Taylor figures out the person responsible for his ill luck: university secretary Flora Carr (Margaret Johnston), wife of a colleague whose career stalled in favor of Norman's. Flora causes his home to go up in flames with Tansy in it. Then, Flora awakens the giant stone eagle on the top of the university building's entrance to attack Taylor.

LENGTH: 90 minutes
RATING: Not rated

2013
JUNE

SU	M	TU	W	TH	F	SA
						1
2	3	4	5	6	7	8 ● 11:56 a
9	10	11	12	13	14 Flag Day	15
16 Father's Day	17	18	19	20	21 Litha/ Summer Solstice	22
23 ☺ Strong Sun Moon, 7:32 a	24	25	26	27	28	29
30						

MOVIE FACT:
This British movie was retitled as Night of the Eagle for the American market.
The story is based on the Fritz Leiber novel Conjure Wife.

Bell, Book, and Candle (1958)

A classic story of Witch Gillian (Kim Novak), who casts a love spell on book editor Shep (Jimmy Stewart) because he is engaged to her college rival. The two then have a whirlwind romance, but he finds out about the spell and gets another Witch to reverse it. When Gillian finds she has lost her powers, she realizes she has fallen in love with Shep. The dilemma is that in this movie, Witches aren't allowed to fall in love. Excellent performances are given by Jack Lemmon as the madcap brother, Elsa Lanchester as the eccentric aunt Queenie, and Ernie Kovacs as an author who wants to write a book about Witches in New York City. Based on the play by John Van Druten.

LENGTH: 106 minutes
RATING: Not rated

2013
JULY

SU	M	TU	W	TH	F	SA
	I	2	3	4 Independence Day	5	6
7	8 ● 3:14 a	9	10	11	12	13
14	15	16	17	18	19	20
21	22 ☺ Blessing Moon, 2:16 p	23	24	25	26	27
28	29	30	31			

MOVIE QUOTE:

Queenie: I sit in the subway sometimes, on buses, or the movies, and I look at the people next to me, and I think, "What would you say if I told you I was a Witch?"

Curse of the Demon (1957)

Based on the M. R. James story "Casting the Runes," this is a subtle and frightening movie. John Holden (Dana Andrews), an American authority on paranormal psychology, arrives in London. He is met by a colleague, who tells him that Henry Harrington, who was investigating Dr. Julian Karswell's "devil cult," was found dead that morning. At the British Museum the next day, Holden retraces Harrington's research and discovers that a critical manuscript is missing. Karswell (Niall MacGinnis) appears and invites Holden to his estate to study his copy of the manuscript. There, Karswell demonstrates his powers by calling down a violent windstorm. After lightning strikes a tree next to Holden, Karswell says that Holden will die unless he stops his investigation. Back at his hotel room Holden finds a parchment with runic writing, which flies out of his hands toward the fireplace. He manages to catch it and learns that Harrington also received such parchment. To reverse the curse and save his life, Holden must give the parchment back to Karswell that very night.

LENGTH: 95 minutes
RATING: Not rated

2013
AUGUST

SU	M	TU	W	TH	F	SA
				1 Lammas	2	3
4	5	6 ● 5:51 p	7	8	9	10
11	12	13	14	15	16	17
18	19	20 ☺ Corn Moon, 9:45 p	21	22	23	24
25	26	27	28	29	30	31

MOVIE QUOTE:
Joanna Harrington: You could learn a lot from children. They believe in things in the dark, although we tell them it's not so. Maybe we've been fooling them.

I Married a Witch (1942)

In 1672, Puritan Jonathan Wooley burned two witches, Jennifer (Veronica Lake) and her father. In revenge, Jennifer cursed all future generations of the Wooley family: the sons will always marry the wrong woman and be miserable. In the twentieth century, a bolt of lightning frees the spirits of Jennifer and her father. Jennifer regains physical form and decides to make Wallace Wooley (Fredric March), Jonathan's unhappily engaged descendent, even more miserable by getting him to fall in love with her before his wedding. Wallace resists, and Jennifer has to resort to a love potion, which backfires with hilarious results. Robert Benchley, the famous humorist, plays Wooley's best friend. There is a major inaccuracy in this movie: no one was ever burned for witchcraft in America. Based on Thorne Smith's novel *The Passionate Witch*.

LENGTH: 77 minutes
RATING: Not rated

2013
SEPTEMBER

SU	M	TU	W	TH	F	SA
1	2 Labor Day	3	4	5 ● 7:36 a	6	7
8	9	10	11	12	13	14
15	16	17	18	19 ☺ Harvest Moon 7:13 a	20	21
22 Mabon/ Fall Equinox	23	24	25	26	27	28
29	30					

MOVIE QUOTE:
Jennifer: Ever hear of the decline and fall of the Roman Empire?
That was our crowd.

The Wizard of Oz (1939)

In this iconic film based on the popular L. Frank Baum book, Dorothy (Judy Garland) and her dog Toto are caught in a tornado's path and end up in the land of Oz. Glinda the Good Witch (Billie Burke) starts her on her journey down the yellow brick road. She meets the Scarecrow (Ray Bolger), the Tin Man (Jack Haley), and the Cowardly Lion (Bert Lahr), who join her in her journey to meet the Wizard of Oz (Frank Morgan). Dorothy wants to get back to Kansas, and her friends want a brain, a heart, and courage. They defeat the Wicked Witch of the West (Margaret Hamilton), and Dorothy does eventually get home. This movie created or re-enforced many modern stereotypes of the Witch: the green skin, the long black dress and pointy hat, and the cackling laugh.

LENGTH: 101 minutes
RATING: Not rated

2013
OCTOBER

SU	M	TU	W	TH	F	SA
		I	2	3	4 ● 8:35 p	5
6	7	8	9	10	II	12
13	14 Columbus Day (observed)	15	16	17	18 ☺ Lunar eclipse Blood Moon, 7:38 p	19
20	21	22	23	24	25	26
27	28	29	30	31 Samhain/ Halloween		

MOVIE QUOTE:
Wicked Witch of the West: Going so soon? I wouldn't hear of it.
Why, my little party's just beginning.

Discussion Questions

1. How accurate or inaccurate do you feel the Witch character in this movie was? Which details were on-target and which were made up? Does this movie use any stereotypes?

2. Was the Witch the protagonist (hero) or the antagonist (enemy)? Who functioned as their opposite? Who triumphed at the end of the film?

3. Did you find the Witch to be a likable character? Could you sympathize with his or her motives? If the Witch was the "bad guy," did he or she have any redeeming qualities? Do you think non-Pagans would feel differently?

2013
NOVEMBER

SU	M	TU	W	TH	F	SA
					1 All Saints' Day	2
3 ● 7:50 a Solar eclipse DST ends, 2 a	4	5 Election Day (general)	6	7	8	9
10	11 Veterans Day	12	13	14	15	16
17 ☺ Mourning Moon, 10:16 a	18	19	20	21	22	23
24	25	26	27	28 Thanksgiving Day	29	30

Movies can and do have tremendous influence in shaping young lives in the realm of entertainment towards the ideals and objectives of normal adulthood.
~Walt Disney

4. When was this movie released? How do you think the movie reflects the ideas of the time in regard to Witches and witchcraft?

5. From a mundane viewer's perspective, did you enjoy the film? Why or why not? Would you watch it again or recommend it to others, Pagan or otherwise?

2013
DECEMBER

SU	M	TU	W	TH	F	SA
1	2 ● 7:22 p	3	4	5	6	7
8	9	10	11	12	13	14
15	16	17 ☻ Long Nights Moon, 4:28 a	18	19	20	21 Yule/ Winter Solstice
22	23	24 Christmas Eve	25 Christmas Day	26	27	28
29	30	31 New Year's Eve				

I don't take movies seriously, and anyone who does is in for a headache.
~Bette Davis

Moon Void-of-Course Data for 2012

JANUARY

Last Aspect Date	Time	New Sign	Sign	New Time
2	3:07 p	2	♉	5:16 p
5	3:46 a	5	♊	5:44 a
7	2:52 p	7	♋	4:05 p
9	9:25 p	9	♌	11:35 p
12	3:23 a	12	♍	4:44 a
13	8:58 p	14	♎	8:28 a
16	10:29 a	16	♏	11:33 a
18	1:31 p	18	♐	2:29 p
20	4:49 p	20	♑	5:40 p
22	8:38 p	22	♒	9:53 p
25	3:33 a	25	♓	4:11 a
26	11:53 p	27	♈	1:28 p
30	1:08 a	30	♉	1:28 a

FEBRUARY

Last Aspect Date	Time	New Sign	Sign	New Time
1	2:06 p	1	♊	2:14 p
4	12:06 a	4	♋	1:04 a
6	7:31 a	6	♌	8:24 a
8	11:42 a	8	♍	12:32 p
10	12:11 a	10	♎	2:54 p
12	4:09 p	12	♏	5:01 p
14	12:04 p	14	♐	7:56 p
16	11:03 p	17	♑	12:03 a
19	4:22 a	19	♒	5:28 a
21	11:17 a	21	♓	12:31 p
22	9:24 p	23	♈	9:48 p
26	7:52 a	26	♉	9:29 a
28	2:46 p	28	♊	10:27 p

MARCH

Last Aspect Date	Time	New Sign	Sign	New Time
2	8:14 a	2	♋	10:08 a
4	5:17 p	4	♌	6:17 p
6	8:27 p	6	♍	10:27 p
8	4:39 a	8	♎	11:50 p
10	10:09 p	11	♏	12:24 a
12	2:30 p	13	♐	2:54 a
15	3:34 a	15	♑	6:24 a
17	9:00 a	17	♒	12:11 p
19	4:31 p	19	♓	8:05 p
21	4:39 a	22	♈	5:57 a
24	1:17 p	24	♉	5:43 p
27	12:35 a	27	♊	6:43 a
29	2:05 p	29	♋	7:07 p

APRIL

Last Aspect Date	Time	New Sign	Sign	New Time
1	12:20 a	1	♌	4:35 a
3	9:47 a	3	♍	9:53 a
5	1:37 a	5	♎	11:32 a
7	6:15 a	7	♏	11:18 a
9	2:56 a	9	♐	11:12 a
11	7:06 a	11	♑	1:02 p
13	1:05 p	13	♒	5:48 p
15	6:42 p	16	♓	1:38 a
17	10:34 a	18	♈	11:59 a
20	3:35 p	21	♉	12:05 a
22	1:10 p	23	♊	1:05 p
25	4:31 p	26	♋	1:42 a
28	3:05 a	28	♌	12:10 p
30	10:17 a	30	♍	7:02 p

MAY

Last Aspect Date	Time	New Sign	Sign	New Time
2	6:58 a	2	♎	10:04 p
4	2:02 p	4	♏	10:20 p
6	8:14 a	6	♐	9:39 p
8	9:34 p	8	♑	10:00 p
10	3:11 p	11	♒	1:03 a
12	8:52 p	13	♓	7:42 a
15	7:59 a	15	♈	5:45 p
17	5:44 p	18	♉	6:03 a
20	8:35 a	20	♊	7:05 p
22	6:51 p	23	♋	7:31 a
25	10:34 a	25	♌	6:11 p
27	7:54 p	28	♍	2:06 a
30	1:50 a	30	♎	6:46 a
31	9:31 p	4/1	♏	8:31 a

JUNE

Last Aspect Date	Time	New Sign	Sign	New Time
3/31	9:31 p	1	♏	8:31 a
3	5:29 a	3	♐	8:32 a
5	1:08 a	5	♑	8:31 a
7	8:38 a	7	♒	10:17 a
9	2:33 p	9	♓	3:22 p
11	6:41 a	12	♈	12:21 a
13	11:09 a	14	♉	12:22 p
16	8:09 a	17	♊	1:24 a
19	11:02 a	19	♋	1:34 p
21	12:48 p	21	♌	11:47 p
23	6:26 p	24	♍	7:42 a
26	6:53 a	26	♎	1:15 p
28	4:22 a	28	♏	4:32 p
30	3:46 p	30	♐	6:04 p

JULY

Last Aspect Date	Time	New Sign	Sign	New Time
2	6:21 p	2	♑	6:51 p
4	8:25 a	4	♒	8:26 p
6	11:49 a	7	♓	12:29 a
8	7:00 a	9	♈	8:14 a
11	5:23 a	11	♉	7:30 p
13	3:46 p	14	♊	8:26 a
16	6:56 a	16	♋	8:31 p
19	12:24 a	19	♌	6:13 a
21	1:17 a	21	♍	1:24 p
22	8:44 p	23	♎	6:38 p
25	11:22 a	25	♏	10:29 p
26	11:38 a	28	♐	1:18 a
29	5:01 p	30	♑	3:29 a
31	7:30 p	8/1	♒	5:56 a

AUGUST

Last Aspect Date	Time	New Sign	Sign	New Time
7/31	7:30 p	1	♒	5:56 a
3	3:24 a	3	♓	9:58 a
5	1:56 p	5	♈	4:59 p
7	4:04 p	8	♉	3:28 a
9	2:55 p	10	♊	4:11 p
12	5:49 p	13	♋	4:27 a
15	4:21 a	15	♌	2:05 p
17	1:55 p	17	♍	8:33 p
18	7:26 p	20	♎	12:45 a
22	3:13 a	22	♏	3:54 a
23	5:34 a	24	♐	6:50 p
26	2:39 a	26	♑	9:58 a
28	6:33 a	28	♒	1:38 p
30	1:48 p	30	♓	6:31 p

SEPTEMBER

Last Aspect Date	Time	New Sign	Sign	New Time
1	4:02 p	2	♈	1:37 a
4	7:06 a	4	♉	11:41 a
5	2:54 p	7	♊	12:10 a
9	6:59 a	9	♋	12:49 p
11	5:58 p	11	♌	11:00 p
14	1:14 a	14	♍	5:30 a
16	7:26 a	16	♎	8:55 a
18	7:30 a	18	♏	10:46 a
20	9:11 a	20	♐	12:34 p
22	12:45 p	22	♑	3:20 p
24	5:19 p	24	♒	7:32 p
26	11:33 p	27	♓	1:23 a
28	10:35 p	29	♈	9:14 a

OCTOBER

Last Aspect Date	Time	New Sign	Sign	New Time
1	6:32 p	1	♉	7:26 p
4	3:44 a	4	♊	7:47 a
5	5:08 p	6	♋	8:45 p
8	3:33 a	9	♌	7:55 a
10	5:40 p	11	♍	3:23 p
12	7:48 p	13	♎	7:02 p
15	8:02 a	15	♏	8:06 p
16	10:23 p	17	♐	8:26 p
19	4:27 p	19	♑	9:41 p
21	11:32 p	22	♒	1:02 a
23	9:27 p	24	♓	7:00 a
26	11:04 a	26	♈	3:31 p
27	9:32 p	29	♉	2:15 a
29	5:01 p	31	♊	2:40 p

NOVEMBER

Last Aspect Date	Time	New Sign	Sign	New Time
2	5:21 a	3	♋	3:43 a
4	3:37 a	5	♌	2:39 p
7	10:27 a	7	♍	11:35 p
9	7:27 p	10	♎	4:35 a
12	12:13 p	12	♏	6:10 a
14	5:39 a	14	♐	5:52 a
16	4:44 a	16	♑	5:35 a
18	12:54 a	18	♒	7:10 a
20	9:31 a	20	♓	11:55 a
22	1:32 a	22	♈	8:12 p
23	8:34 p	25	♉	7:18 a
26	7:57 p	27	♊	7:58 p
28	8:04 p	30	♋	8:55 a

DECEMBER

Last Aspect Date	Time	New Sign	Sign	New Time
2	1:55 a	2	♌	8:57 p
4	5:08 p	5	♍	6:51 a
7	5:35 a	7	♎	1:35 p
9	7:37 p	9	♏	4:51 p
11	8:08 a	11	♐	5:22 p
13	3:42 a	13	♑	4:43 p
15	4:15 p	15	♒	4:53 p
17	1:12 p	17	♓	7:48 p
20	12:19 a	20	♈	2:43 a
22	7:57 a	22	♉	1:25 p
25	12:58 a	25	♊	2:13 a
27	1:50 a	27	♋	3:06 p
28	9:43 a	30	♌	2:45 a
31	4:52 p	1/1	♍	4:48 a

Moon Void-of-Course Data for 2013

Last Aspect		New Sign	
Date	Time	Sign	NewTime

JANUARY

Date	Time	Sign	NewTime
3	7:15 a	3 ♎	8:11 p
5	6:13 p	6 ♏	1:09 a
7	6:31 a	8 ♐	3:28 a
8	9:28 p	10 ♑	3:54 a
11	2:44 p	12 ♒	4:01 a
13	3:37 a	14 ♓	5:49 a
16	4:32 a	16 ♈	11:07 a
18	7:40 p	18 ♉	8:36 p
20	1:16 p	21 ♊	9:04 a
23	6:42 a	23 ♋	10:00 p
25	3:35 p	26 ♌	9:20 a
28	11:59 a	28 ♍	6:27 p
30	8:59 p	31 ♎	1:36 a

FEBRUARY

Date	Time	Sign	NewTime
1	8:03 p	2 ♏	7:02 a
4	7:31 a	4 ♐	10:45 a
5	3:42 p	6 ♑	12:55 p
7	7:44 a	8 ♒	2:16 p
10	2:20 a	10 ♓	4:20 p
11	12:03 p	12 ♈	8:51 p
14	10:35 p	15 ♉	5:08 a
17	3:31 p	17 ♊	4:50 p
19	1:48 p	20 ♋	5:45 a
21	9:08 p	22 ♌	5:12 p
24	11:50 p	25 ♍	1:52 a
26	1:13 p	27 ♎	8:02 a
28	3:37 p	3/1 ♏	12:33 p

MARCH

Date	Time	Sign	NewTime
2/28	3:37 a	1 ♏	12:33 p
3	4:19 a	3 ♐	4:11 p
5	10:28 a	5 ♑	7:14 p
7	4:14 p	7 ♒	10:01 p
8	5:08 p	10 ♓	1:19 a
11	3:51 p	12 ♈	7:17 a
13	4:02 a	14 ♉	3:08 p
16	7:11 p	17 ♊	2:09 a
19	1:27 p	19 ♋	2:55 p
20	2:02 p	22 ♌	2:50 a
22	11:28 p	24 ♍	11:49 a
25	8:46 a	26 ♎	5:32 p
27	2:14 p	28 ♏	8:53 p
29	4:25 p	30 ♐	11:13 p

APRIL

Date	Time	Sign	NewTime
1	1:00 a	2 ♑	1:35 a
3	6:35 a	4 ♒	4:41 a
5	1:22 p	6 ♓	9:00 a
8	12:10 a	8 ♈	3:02 p
10	12:25 p	10 ♉	11:22 p
13	8:30 a	13 ♊	10:13 a
15	3:41 p	15 ♋	10:49 p
18	8:31 a	18 ♌	11:13 a
19	5:06 p	20 ♍	9:08 p
22	2:02 a	23 ♎	3:25 a
24	8:12 a	25 ♏	6:25 a
26	4:56 a	27 ♐	7:32 a
29	12:37 a	29 ♑	8:21 a

MAY

Date	Time	Sign	NewTime
1	10:07 a	1 ♒	10:20 a
3	12:24 a	3 ♓	2:25 p
5	12:00 p	5 ♈	9:03 p
7	8:40 a	8 ♉	6:09 a
9	8:28 p	10 ♊	5:21 p
12	9:32 a	13 ♋	5:57 a
15	8:14 a	15 ♌	6:38 p
18	12:35 a	18 ♍	5:33 a
20	12:48 p	20 ♎	1:07 p
22	3:35 a	22 ♏	4:55 p
24	9:55 a	24 ♐	5:49 p
26	6:22 a	26 ♑	5:28 p
28	2:40 p	28 ♒	5:48 p
30	7:57 p	30 ♓	8:30 p

JUNE

Date	Time	Sign	NewTime
2	12:30 a	2 ♈	2:33 a
4	2:09 a	4 ♉	11:53 a
5	9:25 a	6 ♊	11:32 p
9	4:29 a	9 ♋	12:16 p
10	5:15 p	12 ♌	12:58 a
14	7:14 a	14 ♍	12:26 p
16	5:26 a	16 ♎	9:19 p
18	11:55 p	19 ♏	2:38 a
20	3:16 p	21 ♐	4:31 a
23	3:08 a	23 ♑	4:08 a
24	10:24 p	25 ♒	3:27 a
26	9:08 a	27 ♓	4:32 a
28	8:16 p	29 ♈	9:07 a

JULY

Date	Time	Sign	NewTime
1	2:48 a	1 ♉	5:43 p
3	11:51 a	4 ♊	5:21 a
6	8:30 a	6 ♋	6:14 p
8	7:44 a	9 ♌	6:48 a
11	3:54 p	11 ♍	6:12 p
13	11:26 a	14 ♎	3:41 a
15	11:18 p	16 ♏	10:24 a
18	7:12 a	18 ♐	1:54 p
20	11:00 a	20 ♑	2:39 p
21	11:53 a	22 ♒	2:07 p
23	10:01 a	24 ♓	2:22 p
25	2:43 p	26 ♈	5:29 p
27	10:19 p	29 ♉	12:43 a
30	11:58 a	31 ♊	11:42 a

AUGUST

Date	Time	Sign	NewTime
1	12:48 p	3 ♋	12:29 a
5	2:49 a	5 ♌	12:58 p
6	5:51 p	7 ♍	11:57 p
9	6:05 p	10 ♎	9:08 a
11	9:29 p	12 ♏	4:18 p
14	5:30 p	14 ♐	9:04 p
16	1:32 p	16 ♑	11:25 p
18	2:36 p	19 ♒	12:07 a
20	9:45 p	21 ♓	12:43 a
22	9:38 p	23 ♈	3:13 a
25	6:02 a	25 ♉	9:13 a
26	6:58 a	27 ♊	7:08 p
29	12:44 a	30 ♋	7:33 a
31	8:06 p	9/1 ♌	8:01 a

SEPTEMBER

Date	Time	Sign	NewTime
8/31	8:06 p	1 ♌	8:01 a
3	1:52 p	4 ♍	6:43 a
6	6:10 a	6 ♎	3:12 p
8	4:46 p	8 ♏	9:44 p
10	5:21 a	11 ♐	2:36 a
12	1:08 p	13 ♑	5:56 a
14	7:17 p	15 ♒	8:05 a
16	4:19 a	17 ♓	9:58 a
19	7:13 a	19 ♈	12:58 p
20	9:25 p	21 ♉	6:33 p
23	3:13 a	24 ♊	3:34 a
26	7:21 a	26 ♋	3:24 p
29	3:30 a	29 ♌	3:57 a

OCTOBER

Date	Time	Sign	NewTime
1	12:48 a	1 ♍	2:52 p
3	2:57 p	3 ♎	10:59 p
5	6:28 p	6 ♏	4:33 a
8	12:54 a	8 ♐	8:21 a
10	6:10 a	10 ♑	11:17 a
11	8:04 p	12 ♒	2:00 p
14	4:28 p	14 ♓	5:06 p
16	3:15 a	16 ♈	9:18 p
18	7:38 p	19 ♉	3:27 a
20	5:02 p	21 ♊	12:14 p
22	8:35 p	23 ♋	11:36 p
25	4:31 p	26 ♌	12:12 p
28	8:26 a	28 ♍	11:45 p
30	10:48 p	31 ♎	8:22 a

NOVEMBER

Date	Time	Sign	NewTime
2	8:47 a	2 ♏	1:35 p
3	11:23 p	4 ♐	3:14 p
5	11:48 a	6 ♑	4:44 p
8	2:39 a	8 ♒	6:30 p
10	12:57 p	10 ♓	9:36 p
12	9:34 a	13 ♈	2:39 a
14	3:57 p	15 ♉	9:49 a
17	10:16 a	17 ♊	7:07 p
19	10:59 a	20 ♋	6:23 a
22	2:11 a	22 ♌	6:56 p
24	3:59 a	25 ♍	7:11 a
27	6:44 a	27 ♎	5:00 p
29	6:13 a	29 ♏	11:03 p

DECEMBER

Date	Time	Sign	NewTime
1	8:34 p	2 ♐	1:31 a
3	10:45 p	4 ♑	1:49 a
6	12:31 a	6 ♒	1:53 a
7	7:11 a	8 ♓	3:34 a
10	1:41 a	10 ♈	8:06 a
12	10:37 a	12 ♉	3:40 p
14	9:54 p	15 ♊	1:40 a
17	4:28 a	17 ♋	1:17 p
19	11:37 p	20 ♌	1:48 a
22	8:25 a	22 ♍	2:19 p
24	10:55 p	25 ♎	1:17 a
27	6:00 a	27 ♏	8:58 a
29	8:54 a	29 ♐	12:37 p
30	6:36 a	31 ♑	1:01 a

SET IN EASTERN TIME, CORRECTED FOR DAYLIGHT-SAVING TIME

Llewellyn's 2013 Witches' Line!

Notes:

Notes:

Notes:

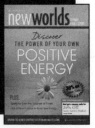